An Inspector Ca

The History and Development of the Children and Family Court Advisory and Support Service

ARRAN POYSER

First published in the United Kingdom in 2024 by

The Choir Press

ISBN 978-1-78963-441-9

Acknowledgements

I am grateful to Karen Harris, administrator at Nagalro, for retrieving articles written by myself and others from its journal, Seen and Heard; to Mavis Maclean CBE, editor of the Journal of Social Welfare Law, for her advice, enthusiasm and encouragement; Professor Mervyn Murch CBE, for his long-standing friendship and wise counsel; and to Dame Joyce Plotnikoff for her support and retrieval of key publications.

Thanks are also due to Cafcass for releasing archived board minutes under its Freedom of Information (FOI) provisions; to District Judge Charles Prest KC and Richard White for help with legal references; and to John Rowlands OBE, Richard White and others for their constructive challenge and unfailing attention to detail.

A number of professionals and former colleagues not only offered their spontaneous recollections about Cafcass and other related topics for use in this project, without being prompted as to what they might refer, but they all also waived the accompanying offer of anonymity. Special thanks are due to Kit Chivers, Susan Cooper, Deidre Correa, Anthony Douglas CBE, Liz Goldthorpe, Azora Hurd, Leonie Jordan, Jim Lawson, Mary Ann McFarlane, Charles Prest, Professor June Thoburn, Judith Timms OBE, Professor Jane Tunstill, Sir William Utting, John Walters, David Walton and Richard White.

Many former professional contacts are not named. Some – indeed far too many – are in poor health or sadly have died. Others, for their own reasons, which are fully respected, may not wish to be identified. But their contribution to many of the events described in this book, often in support of my own particular activities, should not be overlooked. And I thank each of them with all sincerity.

Although a few words of this book's title are derived from J. B. Priestly's 1945 play, there is no other implied connection.

This project could not have come to a successful fruition without the support, professional advice and technical expertise of Miles Bailey, Naomi Music, Rachel Woodman and other colleagues at The Choir Press, to whom heartfelt appreciation is owed. Even so, any factual errors in this account, including of course the many inevitable omissions from such a large canvass, are my sole responsibility.

Contents

Acknowledgements iii

Foreword vi

1. Introduction 1

2. Guardian Service Developments 4

3. The Children Act 1989 23

4. The Future of Welfare Support Services 38

5. Preparing for Cafcass 48

6. Cafcass' First Years 62

7. Cafcass and Later Developments 85

8. The UN Convention on the Rights of the Child 103

9. Family Justice Developments 112

10. Inspectorates 148

11. Departures 176

12. Two Questions 185

13. Past and Future 189

Appendix One 196

Appendix Two 201

Author 202

Foreword

I first met Arran Poyser in 1997, when I was appointed to the secretariat for the Advisory Board on Family Law and its Children Act sub-committee. His extensive knowledge of the subject field was immediately evident, and he made a huge contribution to the work. He was also a supportive and experienced colleague who could be relied on to guide a very new boy through some of the complexities involved with both the subject and the diverse relationships concerned.

Some years later, in 2005, I was appointed HM Chief Inspector of Court Administration for England and Wales. It was a delightful surprise to find Arran in post as a member of the senior management team. Once again I found myself benefiting from his wise counsel and kind support, particularly on inspections of Cafcass, which he led. The work of his team was of such high quality that I invariably found my role was simply to read the report and add my name to it. I should not be surprised, therefore, that the reading of this book has allowed me to repeat that process, with the added privilege of offering this foreword.

This scholarly work comes at a timely moment in the development of the family justice system. Longstanding calls for greater openness and transparency are gradually being addressed. This book, and in particular its chronicling of the creation and development of Cafcass, is an informative adjunct to that process. I commend it to anyone with a personal or professional interest in the family courts and the wider family justice system.

Eddie Bloomfield

HM Chief Inspector of Court Administration (2005–2010) and Public Trustee (2010–2016)

1

Introduction

Among the most difficult questions facing the family justice system in England and Wales is when and how the state should intervene in family life via the courts and when, if it does so, is it as sure as possible that its actions will do more good than harm? Among many other challenges is the need for a better understanding about what works here, how jurisdictions elsewhere around the world deal with similar issues involving family related breakdowns and what of relevance can be learnt from their experience.

This book offers those with an interest in the family justice system, for whatever reason, an overview from an inspectorate standpoint. A selection is made of legal, policy, practice, research and inspectorate milestones that mainly cover the four decades from the mid-1980s through to the 2020s.

During that period, there were many landmarks, but two in particular are given prominence: preparing for and implementing the Children Act 1989 in 1991 and setting up the Children and Family Court Advisory and Support Service (Cafcass) in 2001. The latter explains the book's title.

My own professional involvement with both of these developments, among a number of other responsibilities, spans 23 years as a government inspector. However, I report on some of these wider events more in the role of a spectator than as a direct participant. The latter explains the book's subtitle. Some events pre-date my professional career; other post-date my retirement.

To help better convey the 'voices' of key events and linked opinions, extensive use is made of what was said or written at the time. These are set out as direct quotations – frequently from official sources. Although the language used may sometimes jar for today's reader, it tends to reflect not only the way ideas were expressed some years ago but also the context and sometimes the underlying organisational culture of that period. Footnote references will hopefully be of assistance for anyone wishing to explore these issues in greater detail.

Personal Recollections

Recollections from a number of professionals and former colleagues, as well as my own, are included in several chapters. Contributors are listed in the acknowledgements.

The Voice of the Child

Hearing the voice of the child in the courts took a major step forward in 1984 with the introduction of new system aimed at ensuring there was a clearer focus on what course of action would be best for a child who may have been abused or injured. Guardians ad litem and solicitors would work 'in tandem' to safeguard the interests of the child. The local authority would present its evidence in support of its application, and the child's parents would, if they so wished, give their side of the story. Within this triangle, the court had to decide what happened and whether the evidence satisfied the necessary criteria for making an order or discharging one. In other kinds of proceedings in different courts, parents who were separating or divorcing would be seen by family court welfare officers who would report to the court on, for example, the proposed arrangements for the children.

Court Welfare Support Services

Taking the details of this complex story forward over the following decades, selected departmental and other perspectives focus on describing how the three former court welfare support services operated up to 2001 and what the 1998 departmental consultation on the future of those services proposed. The next stage was the founding legislation that led to Cafcass being established in 2001 as a new organisation covering England and Wales and bringing together more than 140 organisations that made up the former arrangements. Some of the difficulties around setting Cafcass up are explored, as are a selection of other challenges and achievements it experienced during its first years of operation.

Select Committees

Although the Parliamentary Select Committee in 2003 focused on Cafcass difficulties alone, the later Justice Select Committee in 2011 examined both Cafcass and the broader family court system. Both critical reports had key messages for government and wider. Later still came further significant stages with both the Family Justice Review interim and final reports of

2011, as well as the government's response to them both. The main recommendations to these landmark developments were given effect in the Children and Families Act 2014.

The United Nations Convention on the Rights of the Child

The importance of the United Nations Convention on the Rights of the Child (UNCRC), ratified by the UK government in 1992, and its interface with family proceedings is also addressed and is followed by a selection of later developments in the legal, policy and practice approaches taken in some care related and contested private law proceedings.

An Inspectorate Overview

The changing landscape affecting some inspectorates during these years is discussed, as are some key messages arising from inspections of Cafcass.

Other Discussion Areas and Conclusions

The departure of Cafcass' first chief executive and of a Cafcass board member is given some attention. Discussion focuses briefly on two hypothetical scenarios about welfare support service decisions made between 1998 and 2001. After more than two decades of Cafcass operating as a major partner within the family justice system, some wider reflections about governmental and departmental decision-making during this period lead to the book's broader conclusions.

Naming Cafcass

It should be noted that both the acronyms CAFCASS and Cafcass are used, and throughout most of Cafcass' history, source documents are inconsistent in their use of upper and lower case when naming the organisation. This remains so until the present time. However, in this book, for the purpose of consistency, the lower-case acronym will be used, with the exception of quotes, where the acronym will appear in its original form.

2

Guardian Service Developments

This chapter gives an overview of the former family court welfare services, the Office of the Official Solicitor (OS) and the panels of guardians ad litem and reporting officers (Galros). It also covers some research reports and the role of the Department of Health and Social Security (DHSS)[1] in supporting Galro-related developments from 1984 onwards.

The Guardian Ad Litem Concept

Nearly one hundred years ago Parliament legislated about children's interests in the Adoption of Children Act 1926. It said in section 8 that in any application under the Act, the court had to appoint some person or body to act as guardian ad litem (i.e. guardian in the proceedings) of the infant, with the duty of safeguarding the interests of the infant before the court.

Much has happened over the many decades since then to try to ensure that the voice of the child is heard in civil courts dealing with family matters. Language has not always been helpful, with a variety of legal phrases with important but differing nuances, such as 'safeguarding the interests of the child', 'ascertaining the wishes and feelings of the child' and ensuring that 'the child's welfare is the primary consideration'. Added to these are considerations not only about what weight the child's views are given within the judicial decision-making processes, but also how, if and when the child may become a direct actor in such proceedings – and with enforceable rights. Those working with the courts – and the courts themselves – have struggled with these issues. The Court of Appeal has often been called upon to aid clarity. The research community has made numerous high-quality contributions, often helping to influence both government policy and front-line practice.

Among other issues addressed over many years are how, when and by whom independent professional advice – including by a range of experts

[1] In a departmental reorganisation in 1988, the DHSS was split into the Department of Health (DH) and the Department of Social Security (DSS).

– may be given to courts dealing with children in family matters, and also the way different arrangements for service development and delivery have evolved.

Two broad influential streams can be traced that cover both professional practice and organisational service provision. The former has been provided by variously titled front-line practitioners with a mixture of duties, responsibilities and discretionary powers who have worked on an employed or self-employed basis. The latter has a history of changing organisational arrangements. Behind both these activities is the role of Parliament, not only in establishing a legal framework of primary and secondary legislation but also in different ways promoting many of its departmental policies and, where necessary, undertaking detailed parliamentary investigations when serious concerns arise.

Official Solicitor

The Office of Official Solicitor (OS) was established in 1875 to provide confidential advice to civil courts and to represent minors where there were issues of legal or moral complexity central to their welfare. His representation-of-children role was restricted to the High Court and county court levels of the family court structure; in adoption proceedings he only acted in the High Court. Functions were similar to, but not identical with, those of the panel guardians ad litem. The Official Solicitor also had other functions concerning international abductions and the enforcement of child custody orders. Only a proportion of the work of the Official Solicitor concerned children in family proceedings.

Panels

Establishing the guardians ad litem and reporting officer panels began after a delay of nine years, until May 1984, in implementing the section 64 and 65 provisions in the Children Act 1975. These allowed courts to identify certain care-related cases where there was a conflict of interest between a parent and child and to then take steps to separately safeguard the interests of the child by appointing a guardian ad litem to present the child's case. Court rules prescribed the guardian's duties, all of which were aimed at safeguarding the interests of the child. This same Act sets out regulation-making powers in section 103 to establish panels of guardians ad litem and reporting officers. The origins of this legislation arose out of the death of Maria Colwell in 1973 and the subsequent official inquiry published in 1974.[2] The Colwell Committee drew attention to the desirability of an independent social worker's view being available in court proceedings where a local authority is seeking or consenting to a change in the status of a child under their care or supervision.[3]

Post Maria Colwell

Some of the complex issues exercising many in this period are perhaps captured by an article written in 1985[4] that, after its headline, 'Panic Is Not a Solution', included a number of observations, some of which still seem relevant in 2024:

> There is no doubt that the publicity over Maria's death led to this switch in attitudes. Martin Davies, professor of social work at East Anglia University, says: 'Every media exposure means there is a consequential tightening of procedures and also social workers making more effort to cover themselves against criticism.'
>
> But even by the mid-1970s doubts were beginning to emerge about the new tougher policy. Social work is about balancing risks, it was argued, and indignant social workers insisted that assessing those risks should not be the province of journalists, or at the whim of sensational headlines.
>
> They argued that in trying to judge the risk to a child from violent parents, the side of the calculation often forgotten by outsiders was the different sort of damage that can be done to a child by taking it into care. Residential homes are obviously a poor alternative to family life, and perhaps a third of all fostering break down. As Christine Hammond of the British Agencies for Adoption and Fostering says: 'You can make care through adoption and fostering as good as you can, but it is not a real substitute.' And so by the end of the decade the accepted view was that the job of social services was to support children in their homes and to help the family together.
>
> The shape of that support had by then fully evolved: counselling parents about health and housing, teaching them how to discipline and suggesting how to show affection, providing advice and companionship in drop-in centres, finding nursery places for children under five.
>
> Such preventive work, however, means greater risks and also requires able and well-trained social workers, who need to adopt a supportive attitude, but at the same time keep the alertness necessary to spot the potential child-

---

[2] Report of the Committee of Inquiry into the Care and Supervision Provided by Local Authorities and Other Agencies in Relation to Maria Colwell, Chairman: T.G. Field-Fisher, London: HMSO, 1974

[3] Child Abuse – A Study of Inquiry Reports, 1973–1981, DHSS, HMSO, 1982

[4] Brian Deer on the Abuse and Murder of Children – briandeer.com

> killer among the much larger number of parents who abuse in isolated outbursts of anger or frustration.
>
> This is where the system has broken down. In recent years, training has been poor, and tight financial controls on local government have not helped to improve it. Social workers have become 'generalists', dealing with every problem, from old people to the handicapped and delinquent youths. The special problem of child abuse and the specialist skill required to deal with it have been submerged in the deluge of other work.
>
> Now, with the panic beginning to set in again, the balance will inevitably swing back towards the easy solution of taking more children into care. 'If we are being blamed for the fact that the risks don't always work out right, then we will play safe,' says one social work team leader. 'We are bound to think that "this could happen to me" when we see what happens to the social worker involved.'

Establishing Guardian Panels

The duty to establish guardian panels across England and Wales was devolved to local authorities. Two circulars were issued by the Department of Health and Social Security (DHSS) giving guidance on options for how such panels might be established and administered.[5] This guidance in turn led to different service models. Encompassing the 54 panels in England and five panels in Wales, such arrangements included panels run by a single authority, a consortia of several authorities and those contracted out to a voluntary child care organisation.

When working as a senior manager in a London social services department in the early 1980s, I recall:[6]

> *Attending meetings in 1984 to establish the Inner London Galro panel ... and also convening discussion groups offering professional support to departmental colleagues undertaking guardian work in difficult care-related proceedings in other authorities.*

Susan Cooper, who for some years was the chair of the National Association of Guardians Ad Litem and Reporting Officers (Nagalro), suggests several reasons why the government chose to give this responsibility to social services departments (SSDs) despite the inherent difficulties around the lack of perceived independence from one of the parties to the proceedings (i.e. the local authority). These include the hope

[5] LAC 83(21) and LAC 86(2)

[6] 'All in a Day's Work - A Brief Account of my Professional Life: Volume 1', Unpublished Paper, Poyser, A., 2001

of avoiding additional expense; that SSDs already held statutory responsibility for child care matters and were bureaucratically convenient; and that anticipating demand was difficult, as it was impossible to forecast accurately how many guardians would be needed.

Early Guidance

The March 1984 Social Services Committee Second Report commented on the government's announcement that section 64 of the Children Act 1975 was to be implemented in full in the course of 1984. It added at paragraph 106 that:

> Although this will be generally welcomed ... strong reservations were however expressed by the Law Society and the Children's Legal Centre (CLC) ... who fear the result will be a confusion of roles for the guardian, who will be expected both to represent the child's interests but also to an extent to form an independent judgement as an expert witness of what those interests are ... The CLC went so far as to claim that the child's right to a fair hearing would be seriously undermined, and the Law Society saw section 64 increasing rather than diminishing problems over legal representation of children. The British Association of Social Workers (BASW) feared guardians would be 'an unsatisfactory amalgam of advocate, expert witness and inquisitor'.

The Blue Book

Rupert Hughes at the DHSS chaired a consultative working party consisting of himself plus 20 key players drawn from across the field that offered further guidance over and above the court rules and other regulations. This was published in 1984 and was titled the *Guide for Guardians Ad Litem and the Juvenile Courts.* As a shorthand, it was known as the 'Blue Book'. In the section headed 'Independence of the Guardian Ad Litem' the Guide stresses that 'if this person is to be effective in performing his duty to safeguard the welfare of the child, it is essential that he acts, and is seen to act, independently of his employing authority or agency (if he has one) and of the authority administering the panel' and continues to say that 'similarly, he should be free of any previous involvement with the child or family. This is an important principle underlying the court rules which govern the appointment of guardians ad litem.'

The guide also comments on the expertise of a guardian ad litem by stating at paragraph 109 that a qualified social worker appointed as a guardian ad litem may be expected, as a witness, to be accorded the status of an expert on matters of a general social work nature and be able to give expert opinion evidence. He may refer to accepted authorities and research reports, but he may not be entitled to this status in relation to specialist fields such as child abuse and incest unless he can show that he has appropriate specialist expertise. But the guide warns 'his right to be treated as an expert in such areas may be challenged in court'.

The court rules operating then list the seven mandatory duties on guardians ad litem, to which an eighth is whether the juvenile court's final decision should be appealed to the Crown Court. Within the main duties, the second is of particular importance – namely:

> Shall regard as the first and paramount consideration the need to safeguard and promote the infant's best interests until he achieves adulthood, and shall take into account the wishes and feelings of the infant, having regard to his age and understanding, and shall ensure that those wishes and feelings are made known to the court.

Research

Supported by a grant from the DHSS, Bristol University undertook research[7] from July to December 1984 involving interviews across England with 14 local authority panel administrators and 14 justices' clerks. The overall aim of the research was 'to identify possible teething problems associated with implementing the new provisions'. In its conclusions, the authors comment:

> We became increasingly perplexed whether the problems we were uncovering were simply short-term, related to the initial phase, or caused by structural weaknesses in the overall concept. At this stage we are not at all sure that we have reached any satisfactory answer, but perhaps our thinking about the matter will prompt illuminating discussion.

And they add:

> It would be wrong to plunge straight into the more problematic aspects of the scheme without first mentioning the great achievements of all concerned in successfully launching it in a comparatively short time. Only a year ago the DHSS was taking the first steps to prepare the field and was organising a series of regional conferences ... backed up by official circulars and the publication of the 'Blue Book' ... which many people told us they found

[7] 'Separate Representation for Parents and Children: An Examination of the Initial Phase', Murch, M. and Bader, K., University of Bristol Family Law Research Unit, December 1984

> extremely helpful ... many courts became quickly impressed by the initial quality of the GALs' work.

And they further comment:

> None of this could have happened without a great deal of enthusiasm, hard work, and innovative skill on behalf of all concerned. This is even more commendable when one remembers that the scheme was set up at a time when public expenditure was tightly controlled, and was consequently launched at minimum cost ... Many of those involved had obviously given the matter a great deal of thought. The remit had challenged their ingenuity. Bearing in mind that justices' clerks and Social Services Departments were having at the same time to absorb a lot of other legislative change, this was impressive.

The researchers suggest that because it often depends upon which standpoint one adopts as to whether one sees something as a strength or a weakness, they adopt a more neutral approach and focus on two distinctive features which they judge underlie the problem areas – namely, 'diversity of local policy and practice, and ambiguity'. Both are explored in their report.

The research report ends with comments and questions before offering a message of some prescience about service arrangements that would unfold some years in the future:

> The other point that we have been much aware of during the investigation is that we have been studying the beginnings of a new form of court social work service at a time when there is renewed official interest in the idea of Family Courts. The Lord Chancellor's Department and Home Office have established a Family Court Review. When the last such review took place between the Law Commission and the Home Office under the chairmanship of Sir Leslie Scarman, as he then was, the following questions were asked:
>
> 1. Should there be a Family Court with a primary role of adjudication and a clearly defined welfare responsibility?
>
> 2. What should be the extent of the court's welfare enquiry?
>
> Clearly the establishment of the new machinery for GALs is pertinent to such questions. These new types of panel will have to be considered along with the role of the Divorce Court Welfare Service, the role of Reporting Officers and, no doubt, also the various forms of in-court conciliation services which are springing up around the country.

The Green Book

Taking forward some of Murch and Bader's 1984 research, Rupert Hughes chaired a second working group, again with membership widely drawn from the field. It was intended primarily to give advice to local authorities to manage and administer guardian panels and help them provide an effective service to children and the courts. It was also aimed at the courts and court staff involved in appointing guardians ad litem and reporting officers in individual cases. This guide was published by the DHSS in 1988 and titled *Panel Administration.* It was known as the 'Green Book'.

As noted later, both it and the earlier 'Blue Book' guide were withdrawn in 1991 and replaced that year with updated statutory guidance that was necessary when the Children Act 1989 came into force.

Three recommendations covering safeguarding and representing children were made by the *Review of Child Care Law,* more details of which are discussed in Chapter 3. Recommendations 109, 110 and 111 said the child should remain a party, a guardian ad litem should be appointed in each case unless it appears unnecessary to do so in order to safeguard the child's interests, and a lawyer should be appointed to represent the child where 'the guardian ad litem wishes it, or the child is old enough to instruct one himself and wishes to do so, or there is no guardian or the court so directs'.

Other Studies

Two examples of analysis of historical developments around some of these complex and important issues, albeit on different but related topics, are by Mervyn Murch and Douglas Hooper in 1992[8] and by Susan Cooper in 1993.[9]

Murch and Hooper's seminal research was based on findings of a three-year inquiry undertaken from 1987 to 1990. It concerned support services that formed part of the infrastructure associated with the development of the family justice system. It was written at a time when government had committed itself to 'a rolling programme of family law reform, the overall consequences of which are redefining in certain

---

[8] *The Family Justice System,* Murch, M. and Hooper, D., Family Law, 1992

[9] 'Representing the Child: The Evolution of the Guardian Ad Litem in Care Proceedings', Cooper, Susan A.M., Durham theses, Durham University, 1993. Available at Durham E-Theses Online: http://etheses.dur.ac.uk/5682/

profound ways the relationship between social institutions of the family and the law'.

The authors wisely comment on page 66:

> Like all policy issues, in order to find a way forward, it helps to appreciate the history, if only to understand how entrenched some of the protagonists have become and what it is, symbolic or otherwise, that they think they are defending.

They not only mapped key historical developments in the three support services that were operating the early 1990s in advising courts about children's interests, but they also gave a detailed analysis of the pros and cons of possible alternative future support service delivery models, some of which subsequently found expression in the 1998 departmental consultation paper, which is discussed later in Chapter 4.

Susan Cooper's study on the evolution of the guardian ad litem in care proceedings explores issues around representing the child before and after significant changes were introduced through parts of the Children Act 1975 that, as noted earlier, were not implemented until 1984.

Family Court Welfare

In respect of family court welfare, Murch and Hooper explain that following the 1967 Matrimonial Causes Act, probation committees were required to assign a court welfare officer to every divorce county court. Before the implementation of the Children Act 1989 in 1991, the Probation Service's civil work across 54 autonomous areas comprised four functions: inquiry work for the divorce court, mostly involving disputes about custody and access (or residence and contact as they became under the 1989 Act); some inquiry work in the magistrates' domestic court; mediation/conciliation of various kinds; and a little adoption work. The latter became incorporated into the 1984 Galro panel arrangements.

Guidance for the Guardian Service

The Department of Health's statutory guidance for the Guardian Service issued in 1991 is in *The Children Act 1989 Guidance and Regulation Volume 7 Guardians Ad Litem and other Court-related Issues.* My departmental colleague Margaret Vallance and I wrote much of it.

About the same time, two new guides were commissioned by the Department of Health. They were *The Manual of Practice Guidance for*

Guardians Ad Litem and Reporting Officers[10] and *The Manual of Practice Guidance for Galro Panel Managers*.[11] Again, Margaret Vallance and I were the main link with the commissioned authors. These guides not only replaced both the 1984 'Blue Book' and the 1988 'Green Book' but were also able to incorporate much of what had been learnt by the Galro service and the Department of Health in the intervening years.

In her introduction to *The Manual of Practice Guidance*, Judith Timms wrote that the crucial importance of the guardian ad litem's role is that it stands at the interface between the conflicting rights and powers of courts, local authorities and natural and substitute parents in relation to the child. The guardian has to safeguard the child's interests to ensure the most positive outcome for the child. The guardian also has to make a judgement between the potentially conflicting demands of children's rights, children's rescue, the autonomy of the family and the duty of the state. She concludes in terms that, arguably, should still be applicable today: 'Children now move centre stage and guardians ad litem move with them to occupy a pivotal role in the successful implementation of the Act.'

In their introduction to the *Manual of Panel Management*, Henri Giller and Annie Shepperd explain that their aim is to offer practical guidance both to experienced panel managers and to those who have come more recently to the role. They point out that the need for better management of panels had been highlighted by the inspectorate[12] in a 1990 report and was more pressing by the extended range of cases that guardians may be appointed under the Children Act 1989. The manual aims to help panel managers develop good management practices, 'which will ensure that a high-quality Galro service is provided for the courts. In this way the voice of the child will be heard and the interests of the child will be safeguarded and promoted.'

Departmental Support

In addition to the guidance and manuals, there were many other activities led by the Department of Health up to 1999 in support of the Galro service. These spanned financial support, professional guidance for

---

[10] Judith Timms, then the Director of IRCHIN (Independent Representation of Children in Need) was its author.

[11] Henri Giller (Social Information Systems) and Annie Shepperd (Consultant) were its authors.

[12] *In the Interests of Children*, SSI, 1990

practitioners and panel managers, and inspection. I was closely involved in nearly all of them, and they include:

- non-inspection visits to all Galro panels, with detailed follow-up letters
- three formal inspections of selected Galro panels
- developing and publishing *National Standards for the Guardian Ad Litem and Reporting Officer Service (1995)*
- commissioning Social Information Systems Ltd with six Galro panel managers to develop a training pack, *Implementing National Standards*, to aid Galro panel management, followed up with regional training events
- hosting regular regional meetings, organising annual conferences and mounting residential courses for panel managers
- commissioning, with East Sussex County Council, children and a senior family judge, *A Guide to Care Proceeding* for guardians to use with children the subject of care proceedings
- publishing annual overview reports of Galro panel annual reports (1992/3 to 1994/5)
- arranging induction courses for new guardians under the lead of Judith Timms, chief executive of the National Youth Advocacy Service (NYAS)
- running residential induction courses for new Galro panel managers
- convening working parties and reporting on concerning issues (e.g. handling complaints, inter-panel fee-sharing for self-employed guardians, recommended court report format and annual panel report data collection)
- securing a three-year specific grant (1992/3 to 1994/95) totalling £18.4 million to help local authorities with Galro-related costs (LAC (92)2)
- issuing guidance by way of a local authority circular (LAC (94)25) on the guardian's role in reporting under the Human Fertilisation and Embryology Act 1990 in section 30 parental order applications
- circulating regular newsletter updates to all Galro panel managers and panel committee chairs at four- to six-monthly intervals

- attending the President's Interdisciplinary Committee, which eventually became re- formulated as the Family Justice Council[13]
- being the Department of Health member of the working party that prepared the 1998 consultation paper on the future organisation of support services in family proceedings

A further guide for guardians ad litem was commissioned by the Department of Health and published in 1995.[14] It focused on public law proceedings and the professional experience gained by the Guardian Service after the implementation of the Children Act 1989 in 1991.

In respect of organising residential courses for new Galro panel managers, I recall:

> *One was in York and was jointly led by Tess Duncan, Panel Manager Surrey, and myself. After a full day's work, we had arranged a late evening surprise ... a man in a black cape duly appeared at our hotel to conduct us all around the city's dark and narrow streets regaling us with ghostly tales ... it was magnificently spooky!*
>
> *Another course was in Cheltenham where we enjoyed a string quartet recital at the Pump Room.*

Addressing Problems

However, there were many important areas where the Galro service needed to further improve and address certain problems. Examples highlighted below include National Standards, Galro panel annual reports, and complaints.

National Standards for the Galro Service

The National Standards for the Galro service were issued in October 1995 by the Department of Health and Welsh Office in consultation with the Lord Chancellor's Department (LCD) and after discussion within the service.

They had no separate legal identity, but the Department of Health's covering letter explained that 'the standards build on existing statutory requirements, guidance and good professional principles and also reflect the public service principles of the Citizen's Charter' (see later). The letter continued, 'Local authorities and panel committees are invited to review

[13] The Family Justice Council was established in 2004. It is chaired by the president of the Family Division. It is an advisory, non-statutory, non-departmental public body that provides independent expert advice from an interdisciplinary perspective on the operation and reform of the family justice system.

[14] *A Guide for Guardians Ad Litem in Public Law Proceedings Under the Children Act 1989,* Pizzey, S. and Davis, J., HMSO, 1995

their monitoring procedures in the light of this framework. At the local level, the development of other specific standards not covered by the national framework may be desirable. We strongly recommend that performance targets are set and publicized locally.' The aim of the National Standards was to improve the Guardian Service in four ways – namely by:

- setting clear expectations about key areas of required practice, administration and management
- encouraging the delivery of a professionally competent service
- ensuring greater public confidence in the service
- delivering the service consistently, fairly and without improper discrimination.

The 14 National Standards relate to the four main elements of the Guardian Service: the local authority; the management and administration of the service; the panel committee; and the panel of practising guardians. Each standard is introduced with a summary of the legal requirements and followed by examples of relevant supporting criteria that aimed to help the standard be met satisfactorily.

The Citizen's Charter was launched by the then prime minister, John Major, in July 1991. It aimed to improve public services in the UK by making administration accountable and more user-focused, ensuring transparency and the right to information in an open and easy-to-understand manner, taking measures to improve performance in the Civil Service and adopting a stakeholder approach. All public services would have to publish clear targets for levels of service. Those bodies that were meeting their defined standards were granted a 'Charter Mark'. The Charter ensures:

- quality by improving services
- choices for the user standards specifying what to expect within a time frame
- value for the taxpayers' money
- accountability of the service provider
- transparency in rules and procedures
- a proper code of conduct and grievance redressal mechanism

Galro Panel Annual Reports

The requirement that Galro panels should produce annual reports first emerged in the 1991 Children Act Volume 7 statutory guidance.[15] This said the report should include as of the year ending 31 March a summary of the activity of panel members, the breakdown of financial expenditure, the membership of the panel committee, the membership of the panel (i.e. type of Galro and work undertaken by each), training activities, key policy and practice developments, and priorities to be addressed in the period to be covered by the next report. The report should be published in the same year by 30 June.

The first annual report overview[16] states that the panel reports cover a period of rapid change and development and many of them illustrate the considerable extent to which the letter and spirit of the legislative changes have been grasped and implemented. Analysis of the reports reveals both similarities and differences in the way the service is operating and highlights a range of policy and practice issues which will be of wider interest. But the overview also questioned whether the data currently collected by panels provides the most informative basis for understanding how the service is functioning nationally.

Ten suggestions were made about future collections in a detailed annex that raised wider questions about how data was collected and its possible uses both nationally and locally. The annex also announced that the department would set up a working group to report by May 1993 on the inclusion of additional collections and definitions. This report set out 13 schedules as a minimum statistical collection, and further advice was offered in Appendix 9 of the overview of annual reports 1993/1994.

The fourth overview of annual reports for 1994/1995, like its predecessors, offered a range of detailed statistical information and a broad picture of issues addressed by local panels. These were about panel management, panel members and court activity, as well as policy and practice developments. Departmental pressures and competing priorities regrettably resulted in plans for further annual reports being abandoned.

---

[15] Paragraph 2.85

[16] The Children Act 1989 – Galro Annual Reports (1991–1992), An Overview, Department of Health, 1992

Complaints

In 1996 I convened a working party to look at the operation of the complaints' procedures for the Galro service across England and Wales to identify good procedural models for wider dissemination and to make recommendations. Informed by an inspectorate survey about the volume and source of complaints and a Nagalro survey about its guardian members' experience of complaints, the main thrust of the report and its recommendations addressed some of the difficulties arising from the operation of the 1991 panel regulations.[17]

Although there was continuing importance about complaints, particularly from the public service users as a measure of quality assurance, a shift of approach was needed so that a higher proportion of concerns were satisfactorily resolved without recourse to a complaints board. There was also a need for the first time for a clear separation between concerns about professional practice and those relating to serious disciplinary conduct. However, a departmental commitment to amend the panel regulations was overtaken by the May 1997 general election and instead became but one of many issues eventually taken forward to be dealt with by Cafcass.

Problem-solving

My frequent contact with Galro panel managers and senior family judiciary sometimes allowed potential or real difficulties to be resolved, for example by highlighting how problems that had arisen elsewhere had been resolved. I recall:

> *One Galro panel manager being instructed by the director of social services that all Galro correspondence should in future be on county council headed notepaper complete with its coat of arms. I responded to the panel manager's concerns and explained that although the director was acting within his powers, our departmental guidance that tried to ensure a perception of independence would be at risk of being undermined. The panel manager shared my letter with the director, who chose to withdraw his instruction.*

I also recall:

> *A senior judge hearing an appeal arising from family proceedings sending me his draft judgment and asking if it would cause any problems for the*

[17] SI 1991 No. 2051

department and the Galro service. I wrote a letter of thanks and gave an assurance that no difficulties would arise if he went ahead as planned.

Serious Concerns

Writing in 2001,[18] I outlined some serious concerns within the Galro service that had arisen since 1984. For example, one panel manager had a background in residential care and had studied criminology. Although his Galro post did not involve direct client access, it was discovered that he had a long history of serious child abuse in children's homes and he was sentenced to 18 years imprisonment.[19]

Elsewhere, a guardian was highly regarded and achieved some academic distinction for work at an English university on interviewing children. The panel manager discussed her concerns with me at the Department of Health, but no formal evidence was forthcoming. Eventually, the guardian was arrested by police and charged with child abuse offences that dated back to his pre-guardian work at a children's home. He committed suicide the day before he was due to appear in court. Later an inquiry was set up and chaired by a former director of social services with a distinguished legal background. The management of the local Galro service emerged with little criticism.

A very small number of guardians handled their expenses claims dishonestly and were usually dismissed, although one or two served prison sentences. Two other guardians committed suicide, which left unproven suspicions but also concerns. I wrote:[20]

> All this led to much heart searching within the guardian service about the need for extensive financial scrutiny and other checks about practice as well as more rigorous recruitment procedures.

As I wrote in 2001:

> But more generally in my experience, local authorities were reluctant to investigate or cooperate with the DH on the basis that there had been no complaint. They were resistant to my insistence that proper enquiries were needed to establish whether or not there were grounds for concern – it could not safely be pre-judged.

---

[18] Op. cit. 6

[19] https://www.independent.co.uk/news/social-services-chief-jailed-for-20-years-abuse-1271615.html

[20] Op. cit. 6

Annual Workshop

This chapter concludes by referring in detail to the January 1998 London workshop – the seventh – that in many ways set the scene for the events that are covered in the next chapter. The day was titled 'Approaching the Millenium – Children and the Guardian Service Within the Family Justice System'.[21] Some panel managers and I planned it, and attendees included panel managers, panel committee chairs, young people and invited guests from across England and Wales. The day's aims were 'to address the place of children and the Guardian Service within the family justice system – historically, currently and in the future'.

Opening Remarks

In his opening remarks as the workshop chair, Nicholas Crichton from the Inner London Juvenile Court, said of the workshops: 'They afforded a valuable opportunity ... to communicate with each other. After all, because there were 60 panels did not mean that there had to be 60 different ways of doing things.' He went on to suggest that 'the best we could hope for today was a government statement in the coming weeks announcing that there would indeed be a Green Paper on support services and the family courts. Then, there would no doubt be a frenzy of consultative activity, so any clear thinking such as the opportunity today provided would be useful ... that was why those planning today's event had rightly chosen to look to "Approaching the Millenium" as an apt title.'

Keynote Paper

Professor Mervyn Murch's keynote paper addressed some basic questions I had posed, such as what is the family justice system, where has it come from and where does it need to go? In a masterful historical summary, he said:

> The story since the 1960s of the development of English family law and the emergence of a reasonably coherent family justice system is one of a struggle to first define family law as a distinct system of civil jurisprudence, and then to reorder its various components within a single framework of judicial administration. This has been a difficult political task – which continues – because different aspects of family law have different historical origins, because our legal institutions and practitioners are cautious by nature and in the past were inclined to resist change and because whole number of

[21] Report published by the Department of Health, April 1998

> vested interests have built up around particular aspects of family law (divorce, adoption, child protection, etc.) – not just lawyers, the dominant profession within the system, but newer social work professional sub-groups.

He went on to comment about 'professional tribalism' and the emergence of single-disciplinary 'ghettos', which in his view 'complicate the task of interprofessional collaboration' and also 'make it more difficult for the various tribes to see what they have in common and how they fit into the broader picture'. Professor Murch also referred back to some key messages from the 1974 Finer Report,[22] including:

- 'The fundamental principle which must govern the family court is that it should be a judicial institution which, in dealing with family matters, does justice according to law.'
- 'The court must remain and be seen to remain impartial.'
- 'The object of achieving welfare must not be permitted to weaken or shortcut the normal safeguards of judicial process.'
- 'The court must not see the men, women and children with whom it is concerned as "clients" and still less as "patients" for whom the courts is one form of, or a preliminary to, "treatment".'

Readers may well debate whether any of the above comments from 1974 are still of relevance today. For the future, Professor Murch suggested the core welfare support service should become 'a far more efficient, cost-effective, child-sensitive and administratively integrated family justice system … and using a proper modern management system to identify where delays occur'.

Turning to delay in family proceedings, about which so much has been written over so many decades, Professor Murch discussed three key issues in the context of the Children Act 1989:

- 'There are virtually no incentives or rewards for practitioners and courts to conduct their business more economically and expeditiously.'
- 'Paradoxically, the more sophisticated the machinery of family justice becomes, the more elaborate and slower the process.'
- 'The "culture" of the English family justice system is still too adversarial and dominated by the legal cast of mind.'

[22] The Finer Report on One-Parent Families, Cmnd 5629, 1974

Further Presentations

The annual workshop continued with a paper by Maria Ruegger from De Montford University reporting on her study that aimed at discovering 'what sense children make of the guardian ad litem service and how guardians balance children's rights to have their wishes respected with their rights to have their best interests protected'. The address by Dr Maureen Oakley from Warwick University was about her research on the representation of children in active public law proceedings. Anna Faulkner – Galro panel manager, Inner and North London – provided a brief overview of key landmarks from 1984 before discussing 'uncharted waters of the future'.

The workshop also included a children's presentation by a young persons' panel from the National Youth Advocacy Service, small workshop discussions highlighting current strengths and weaknesses, plenary discussion, and a paper by Julie Morgan, who had been elected MP for Cardiff North in May 1997 and was a professionally qualified social worker. She warned that young peoples' voices were not heard by Parliament but that guardian work was at the cutting edge – guardians saw what was happening to children at a critical time in their lives, and guardians had considerable power, as evidenced by the high percentage of their recommendations being accepted in court.

3

The Children Act 1989

This chapter outlines the background for reform in child care law and the subsequent review established by the government which led to the Children Act 1989 being implemented in 1991. It also briefly mentions adoption legislation.

The Need for Reform

Among many policy responsibilities for children in the early 1980s, several were split across three government departments. For example, children's health, children in care and children the subject of care- or adoption-related proceedings came under the Department of Health and Social Security (DHSS). Children's education at both primary and secondary levels, including some children with special needs, came within the remit of the Department for Education (DfE). Children who offended came mainly under the Home Office (HO), as did some arrangements for those children whose parents were separating or divorcing and where the Lord Chancellor's Department had the lead on civil-court-related matters. This confusing picture had arisen mainly from a pattern of piecemeal legislation both pre- and post-Second World War.

Based on conference papers presented in 1998 – from a conference I attended – and later published by the National Institute of Social Work (NISW) in 1999, several highly distinguished authors contribute to a powerful 1948 to 1998 overview. The occasion was to mark 50 years since the passing of the Children Act 1948[1] – another landmark piece of legislation about children.[2] Considering the time when he was then the director of social services for an Inner London local authority, William ('Bill') Utting said:[3]

> *By 1980 I was so concerned about the way in which children in the public care were brought up that I opened discussion of the subject with directors of social services. Much contemporary thought and practice in child care still*

[1] https://docs.scie-socialcareonline.org.uk/fulltext/niswchildcare.pdf

[2] For a valuable overview, see *Child Care Revisited: The Children's Departments* 1948–1971, Chapter 1, Holman, R., 1998

[3] Ibid. page 38

> *lagged behind the legal requirement to take account of the wishes and feelings of children in care in coming to decisions about them. Promoting the constructive participation of young people in their programmes of care seemed to be the most exciting development in prospect. I was haunted by the comment a care leaver made to a working party:*
>
> *'When I look back at it all I think that I was a bit of a problem and was passed from one place to another until I became more of a problem. Yet it was them that made me who I was. I wonder who was the problem, them and their way of doing things, or me?'*

As noted in Chapter 10, Sir William Utting was appointed the first chief inspector of the Social Services Inspectorate, which was established in 1985.

Select Committee Report

The urgent need for reform was taken forward by the Social Services Committee Second Report: Session 1983–84[4] of March 1984, titled 'Children in Care', although it first warned:

> While the law changes slowly to meet new situations and to respond to new ways of looking at society, society itself remains remarkably and depressingly constant in the way in which children are treated and mistreated.

In respect of the slow implementation of child care law, the committee also warned that it makes it:

> Difficult even for outside professional bodies to keep abreast of the law. For children and families directly affected it must be impossible. We strongly recommend that in future whenever possible child care law be spared a process of implementation in drips and drabs.

Arising from the Social Services Committee Second Report: Session 1983–84, the government response was presented to Parliament in July 1984.[5] By then it was able to state that 'the government accepts now the need for a codification of child care law and that an interdepartmental working party has been set up in association with the Law Commission'.

Working Party

A DHSS-led working party was established with the following terms of reference:

---

[4] Paragraph 10, 360–1, HMSO, 1984

[5] Cmnd 9298, HMSO, London

> In the light of the Report of the Social Services Select Committee on Children in Care and of evidence given to the Committee and other relevant material to make proposals and set out options for codification and amendments of child care law.

The working party was led by Rupert Hughes, who was appointed assistant secretary in the Child Care Division at the DHSS. As mentioned elsewhere, he also played an important role in a number of other significant developments. *The Review of Child Care Law*[6] reported in 1985 was as a consultative document making 223 wide-ranging recommendations. Subsequently, many of the *Review of Child Care Law* recommendations were carried forward into the Children Bill, which in turn emerged as the Children Act 1989.

Membership

Crucially, membership of the working party included Professor Brenda Hoggett, Law Commissioner, whose 1998 published work[7]on the law around guardianship was to heavily influence the Children Act 1989 and especially the paramount welfare-of-the-child principle as set out in section 1 of the Act:

> 1. Welfare of the child.
> (a) When a court determines any question with respect to—
> (b the upbringing of a child; or
> (c) the administration of a child's property or the application of any income arising from it, the child's welfare shall be the court's paramount consideration.

Her distinguished legal career, later as a judge and as Baroness Hale of Richmond, eventually led to her serving as president of the Supreme Court of Great Britain from 2017 until her retirement in 2020.[8]

Leadership

Unusually, compared with many in the Senior Civil Service, Rupert Hughes remained in the same post for 11 years. This gave him a range of authoritative insights into complex children and family policy issues. Under Hughes' leadership, the department also developed and

---

[6] *Review of Child Care Law: Report to Ministers of an Interdepartmental Working Party*, HMSO, September 1985

[7] https://assets.publishing.service.gov.uk/media/5a7c11b5ed915d1c30daa606/0594.pdf

[8] *Spider Woman: A Life*, Lady Hale, Bodley Head, 2021

maintained strong links with the field, other government departments, the research community and the senior family judiciary.

Rupert Hughes had a leading role during the passage of the Children Bill through all its parliamentary stages.[9] He oversaw the 10 volumes of statutory guidance covering the Act's provisions and subordinate legislation (i.e. regulations) that were issued in 1991 to coincide with the Act's implementation. He also commissioned a large programme of 24 Department of Health-sponsored research studies evaluating many aspects of the Act. I recall:

> *Rupert Hughes and I attending a meeting with senior civil servants from other government departments. One of the agenda items was to decide the start date for the new Act. Someone with a keen sense of history suggested mid-October and the anniversary of the Battle of Hastings. Since 14 October 1991 was a Monday, this was the date that was agreed.*

Commenting on aspects of the Act after its implementation, Rupert Hughes said:

> *These supportive … [local authority] services are provided irrespective of any court processes. There is no provision (this was considered in Parliament but rejected) for the possibilities of supportive/preventive work with the child at home to be exhausted before a court order authorises the removal. If the child is judged to be at risk of significant harm, then action to protect the child is urgent. There is here, of course, the eternal social work dilemma of how long to leave a child in an unsatisfactory and potentially risky situation – this is a professional problem which legislation cannot solve.*

Rupert Hughes was also a skilled delegator and trusted a small group of his departmental colleagues – of whom I was one – to deliver projects, and often within required tight time limits.

Children Act Guidance

Updated statutory guidance in 1991 was needed, because as well as amending parts of earlier legislation, the Children Act 1989 also repealed seven other acts entirely.[10] Two where I was involved in writing some of the statutory guidance[11] and/or the regulations are briefly mentioned below.

[9] 'Rupert Hughes: Unsung Architect of the Children Act 1989' *Seen and Heard,* Volume 26, Issue 1, Poyser, A., 2016

[10] Schedule 15

[11] Statutory guidance is issued to local authorities under section 7 of the Local Authority Social Services Act 1970 which states 'Local authorities shall, in the exercise of their social services functions, including the exercise of any discretion conferred by any relevant enactment, act under the general guidance of the Secretary of State'.

Residential Care

The regulations and guidance concerned with the care of children in residential homes of various kinds is set out in Volume 4 of the Children Act. The challenge that my departmental colleague and I faced was adapting the former legislative framework that was 20 years old. He brought to the discussion his considerable experience of managing residential care in the voluntary sector. We had the opportunity to adopt a radically new approach to what the principles of the Children Act required. Although the administrative arrangements for the different kinds of homes governed by the regulations[12] are different, the aim is that the requirements with regard to the welfare of each child in the home and the conduct of the home should be subject to the same standards of provision and child care practices. Our proposals were accepted by the departmental policy lead and were given statutory force in the Children's Homes Regulations 1991[13] and the accompanying guidance.

Independent Visitors

The task of writing the guidance concerning the appointment of independent visitors also came to my desk. Although on this topic I did not work with another departmental colleague, I was able to discuss my draft text with key agencies in the field, where it was met with broad approval. The guidance is included in both Volume 3 (Family Placements) and Volume 4 (Residential Care).

Research Overview

The year 2001 saw the publication of a key report[14] that provided an invaluable major overview of the 24 research studies as well as other inspectorate reports and studies. The authors were assisted by a 25-strong advisory group drawn from the Department of Health, the Social Services Inspectorate, local authorities, academia and the voluntary sector.

Training Challenges

Having co-led courses for social workers about child care law during the early 1980s with Rachel Foster at the London Boroughs' Training Committee (LBTC), I was aware of the huge training challenges that the

---

[12] Volume 4, paragraph 1.9 gives guidance on the different names and definitions of these homes.

[13] SI 1991 No. 1506

[14] *The Children Act Now: Messages from Research,* The Stationery Office, 2001

Children Act would pose for social services departments. Writing in 2001[15] about my time in the early 1980s as a social services departmental senior manager, I said:

> I was deeply concerned at the poor knowledge of key child care law exhibited by even senior staff. Also a worry was that they often had none of the authoritative legal texts such as the Acts or publications such as *Clarke Hall & Morrison on Children*. In one authority I persuaded the director to buy these books for all the area offices; in another the only copies were in the director's office. The attitude that 'law was for lawyers, not social workers' was deplorable and accounts in part for the lack of understanding about both children's and parents' rights and the frequency where 'local law' (i.e. custom and practice) overrode the statute.

I was therefore keen to play a full part in a new Children Act 1989 training initiative as an active Department of Health 'observer'.

Training Together

Baroness Faithfull OBE[16] explained the wider context in her preface to Training Together:[17]

> In Autumn 1991, we will be working within the most substantial reform of children's legislation for decades. The new Children Act will have the widest implications for child care polices and practice not only in social services departments but also in education, probation, health and voluntary agencies. Lawyers and courts will be involved with these new approaches in quite new ways, with radical changes to court orders, processes and venues. Such a reform has far-reaching training implications – indeed, without effective training the intentions underpinning the Act cannot be realised. This was recognised by the Family and Child Care law Training Group early in 1986.
>
> This Group's first report, 'Training for Change: Planning an Inter-Agency Framework' was published in September 1988. It was titled an Interim Report. Although focussed on London, the Report was in demand throughout the country and rapidly sold out. The wide dissemination showed the value of such early work on training strategies and the Group's aim remains – to help training and service providing agencies to be prepared for the new

[15] Op. cit. 6

[16] Lucy Faithfull, Baroness Faithfull, OBE (1910–1996) was a British social worker and children's campaigner. She was appointed Oxford City Council's Director of Social Services in 1970. In 1976 she accepted a life peerage and was instrumental in the passing of the Children Act 1989.

[17] 'Training Together: A Training and Curriculum Model for the Children Act 1989', The Family and Child Care Law Training Group, London, November 1989. It was published by LBTC and the London Boroughs' Children's Regional Planning Committee with the addition financial support of the Central Council for the Education and Training of Social Work (CCETSW).

> legislation by suggesting a framework for planning training. The Interim Report was intended to stimulate discussion, to encourage the mobilising of enthusiasm and determination across London, and to obtain the necessary training resources.

Her preface continues:

> It is now necessary and practical to extend the strategic thinking and analyse each section of the Act for its particular training implications for each professional group ... This report sets out a framework which will be of assistance to all agencies in planning and training. In particular, it offers a method of calculating how many staff and which staff will require what kind of training, for how long and when. It looks to three levels of training – Foundation, Comprehensive and Specialist and provides calculations as to the likely costs of such training.

Membership of the Family and Child Care Law Training Group had strong representation from the voluntary and statutory sectors, with nearly 25 professionals involved. The joint conveyors were Peter Riches (Director LBTC) and Jim Richards (Senior Development Officer of the London Boroughs' Children's Regional Planning Committee). Later Rupert Hughes arranged for copies of the report to be sent to all local authorities in England and Wales.

Further Training

Other aspects of preparation for the Children Act in London and further afield, such as in Wales, included many training sessions, where I often co-trained with Leonie Jordan, a lawyer who later in 2001 was appointed to the Cafcass Board. Other training about the Act that I arranged were courtroom 'role plays' with court clerks, lawyers and social workers using the draft court application forms and new criteria for different kinds of applications. I wrote of those events:[18]

> It put everyone on an immediate learning curve, but in the most co-operative, interprofessional manner. Liz Thompson, the senior justices' clerk, gave it her full support, as indeed she did with many other interdisciplinary projects over the years.

Reporting to Court

Another training initiative by the Department of Health was to commission a guide for local authorities to help social workers prepare

[18] Op. cit. 6

statements in care-related proceedings and to prepare appropriate reports for court.[19] I wanted to update a publication that Jim Richards had led on in the mid-1980s for the then DHSS. This was aimed at helping social workers write reports in care proceeding. As noted earlier, at that time Jim Richards was senior development officer for the London Regional Children's Planning Committee.

Joyce Plotnikoff and Richard Wolfson's two pages of acknowledgements in their handbook, *Reporting to Court Under the Children Act 1989*, demonstrate the care taken by them to ensure the advice within its 90 pages was professionally sound and legally accurate. The senior family judiciary offered comment on the draft text. I chaired the project's reference group. His Honour Judge Mark Hedley comments in his preface:

> Over the last few years there has been a significant change in the practice of civil court. The traditional dependence on oral evidence has been replaced by an increasing emphasis on setting out cases in writing, with consequent curbs on such evidence. Alongside this has gone a new level of scrutiny of local authority plans and the giving of much greater importance to the maintenance of contact between children and their natural families. All this requires early and careful thought by social work practitioners.

And he adds:

> Giving evidence or writing a report for court is a specialist skill that is not acquired merely through general social work experience.

And he concludes:

> This is a Handbook for daily use, not an impressive volume for bookcase decoration. It is written with the needs of the busy (and even nervous) practitioner in mind.

To promote the use of the handbook, the Department of Health sponsored 10 regional workshops across England, in which the authors played a full part. I attended them all. Each local authority was invited to send a team comprising a senior manager, a team manager, a trainer and a legal adviser. These workshops used group discussions to tease out major issues for the field. Their messages were collated and published in February 1997 by the Department of Health in a special supplement to *Children Act News*.

---

[19] *Reporting to Court under the Children Act: A Handbook for Social Services*, Plotnikoff, J. and Woolfson, R., HMSO, 1996

Children Act Reports

Required under section 83 of the Children Act 1989, the first Children Act report for Parliament[20,21] in 1992 summarises in Chapter 9 the 1991 departmental launch of its Training Strategy for the Personal Social Services. This was increased by £10.4 million for 1991/92, rising to £19.6 million in 1993/94. The report explains that for 1990/91 a £2.5 million grant was added in respect of training for the implementation of the Children Act 1989.

Chapter 8 of the same report gives a comprehensive and generally positive account of the guardians ad litem and reporting officer service, to which I contributed, as I also did to further Children Act reports. This first report was followed by composite ones for years 1992/93, 1993/4 and 1994/5.

Difficulties

A new senior Department of Health appointee then decided that no more were needed, arguing that many of the statistics were published by other routes for those who wanted to know. My strong objections were brushed aside. However, the Health Select Committee report published on 1 July 1998 was highly critical, stating:[22]

> We were very disturbed to learn that the DoH has over a number of years simply disregarded the statutory requirement that it submit an annual report to Parliament on the working of the Children Act. It should not have been necessary for us to remind the DoH of its duty to obey the law. This does not inspire confidence in the DoH's ability to monitor and enforce local compliance with statutory provisions. It is particularly regrettable in the light of the fact that, back in 1994, the existence of an annual report to Parliament was referred to by the Government in its first report to the UN Committee on the Rights of the Child as evidence that 'the operation of the Children Act and its effect on children is subject to regular and public scrutiny'.

Writing in 2001,[23] I said:

> Luckily, I had obtained a draft copy of the committee's report and was able rapidly to set up arrangements for a report to be written so that the Secretary of State could truthfully say when the committee report went public that steps had already been taken to prepare the next report.

[20] Cm 2144, London, HMSO, February 1993
[21] https://assets.publishing.service.gov.uk/media/5a758a9040f0b6397f35f37f/2144.pdf
[22] House of Commons - Health - Second Report (parliament.uk)
[23] Op. cit. 6

Commenting on some of the difficulties the report's preparation posed, I also wrote in 2001:

> It was not that simple, as it was required to cover the period 1995 to 1999, to take account of Wales, which was in the process of devolving, and include contributions from other government departments, such as the Lord Chancellor's Department for the private law side of the Act and the Department for Education and Employment for the under 8s and day care, to whom responsibility under the Act had been transferred the previous year.

And I added:

> Although one plan was agreed, a further change in senior management in the Department of Health led to a radically different one intended to reflect the 'Quality Protects' programme that had been launched in 1998/89 to improve children's services and the government's objectives for 'Children Looked After' (1999).
>
> Eventually, and not without acrimony, the report was ready to be published. To meet proofreading deadlines, I had to work several nights until 10 or 11 pm, with the printer at the end of the fax and telephone in East London. Much credit for the statistics and general quality of the report must go to my colleagues. One or two MPs referred to the report in subsequent parliamentary debates as 'magnificent' and 'very helpful'.

Further Reports

The Children Act report covering the years 1995 to 1999 was published in January 2000.[24] It is a substantial and comprehensive 153-page document. In contrast, the 2000 report published in July 2001 is a rather slimmer 127-page production, reflecting yet a further change in approach by senior management in the Department of Health.

Chapter 12 of the 2000 report shows orders made annually in England and Wales in private law proceedings from 1993 to 2000 and goes on to explain that:

> From 1993 to 1996 residence orders rose from just over 22,300 to over 27,600. Numbers then declined for two years but rose back up to stand at just over 25,800 in 2000. The number of contact orders have fluctuated since 1993 with the highest recorded in 2000 of 46,700. The number of orders for prohibited steps and specific issues have not shown great variation since 1993, though both have been on an upward trend since 1998.

[24] Cm 4579, TSO

Orders made in public law for England and Wales are also summarised with the added comments that:

> Generally, since 1993 orders for emergency protection were around 2,500 per year with a peak of just over 3,000 for 1994 and 1995. In 1999 the figure dropped to just over 1,500 but rose to just over 2,200 in 2000. Secure accommodation orders have shown annual variations from between 676 to 1,240. Orders for care and supervision rose sharply after the implementation of the Act from around 4,000 in 1993 to about 5,500 in 1994. The number of orders made in 2000 at 7,624 showed a 55% increase on 1999's figures of 4,911.

The report does not attempt to explain any of the factors that may have played a part in such variations. Such an analysis, even if attempted, would have been complex and lengthy and better suited to a separate, detailed research report. Such an initiative, if followed, may have helped reach a better understanding of what safe conclusions, if any, might be drawn. But this will always be difficult given the wide number of, and variation in, local factors involved. The wider issue of government and Cafcass data availability, presentation and interpretation is mentioned briefly at the end of Chapter 6.

National Standards

The National Standards for Probation Service Family Court Welfare were published by the Home Office in 1994 and were issued in consultation with the Lord Chancellor's Department, the Department of Health and the Welsh Office. In a written answer in Parliament 1994, Mr Boateng explained:

> They set out basic standards of good practice, Probation Services should ensure that local procedures are instituted to monitor whether the standards are being achieved. Her Majesty's Inspectorate of Probation inspect service performance against the standards. Court welfare officers must ensure that their work is free from improper discrimination on any ground; chapter one of the standards includes guidance on equal opportunities. In addition, an induction manual produced by the Association of Chief Officers of Probation is given to members of staff on appointment as family court officers and is supported by a National Induction programme and two training resource packs, one of which includes an anti-discriminatory trigger training video.

Advisory Committee

During the passage of the Children Bill through Parliament, a commitment was given by ministers to establish a body to monitor the operation of the Act and to advise them on issues arising from its implementation. It did not have a statutory function. The terms of reference of the Children Act Advisory Committee were announced by the Lord Chancellor on 25 March 1991 as:

> To advise the Lord Chancellor, the Home Secretary, the Secretary of State for Health and the President of the Family Division on whether the guiding principle of the Children Act 1989 are being achieved and whether the court procedures and the guardian ad litem system are operating satisfactorily.

The committee was initially chaired by the Honourable Mrs Justice Booth[25] and later by the Honourable Mrs Justice Bracewell. Its published annual reports commence in 1991/92 and continue to its final report in 1997. They contain a wealth of invaluable information and also raise concerns, such as those about delay. At the same time as its final report, the advisory committee also published the *Handbook of Best Practice in Children Act Cases*. Its introduction states:

> The basic message of this Handbook is that the earlier matters are considered and acted upon by the parties and their advisers, and the more that can be done jointly with other parties, the better the court process can serve the interests of children.

The committee ceased operation on 30 June 1997.

Advisory Board

The Advisory Board on Family Law was set up by the then Lord Chancellor, Lord Mackay of Clashfern, to oversee implementation of the Family Law Act 1996 and included a remit to maintain an overview of the working of the policies embodied in the Children Act within the family court system. Coordination of Children Act work at local level across England and Wales continued by the established network of family court business committees and family court forums.

Another report published in this period (1996) was by Dame Margaret Booth on delay in public and private law proceedings. She made a number of recommendations for the judiciary, the magistracy, the

[25] Dame Margaret Booth was another senior family judge with whom I worked professionally. After her retirement I remained in touch with her until shortly before her death in January 2021.

administration, and other professionals working in this area. These include the need for improved interdisciplinary communication, improved training, enhanced judicial management, improved court administration and improved practices and procedures for transfers (i.e. of proceedings between different tiers of courts).

Adoption

The Children Act 1989 did not deal with adoption matters, as a review of adoption law was already underway. Unlike the 1989 Act (except in relation to childminding and day care), the Adoption and Children Act 2002 not only covered England and Wales but also extended to Scotland. The Act repealed most of the 1976 Adoption Act, and the explanatory notes[26] comment further:

> The purpose of the Act is to reform adoption law, to implement the proposals in the White Paper that require primary legislation, and to underpin the Government's programme to improve the performance of the adoption service and promote greater use of adoption. The Act builds on and incorporates the proposals to update adoption legislation set out in the draft Bill published for consultation in 1996 (*Adoption – A Service for Children;* Department of Health and Welsh Office, March 1996), which were themselves the product of the *Review of Adoption Law,* Department of Health and Welsh Office, October 1992, and the White Paper – *Adoption: The Future*; Cm 2288, November 1993.)

Twenty-one Years On

A major stocktake on the Children Act 1989 was published in 2010 to mark 21 years of royal assent to the Act.[27] The joint opening editorials to the two volumes by guest editors Rupert Hughes and Wendy Rose are followed by 16 papers from 23 distinguished authors. Both editors had left the Department of Health well before 2010, where they had been close colleagues.

> We have sought a wide range of contributors for these special editions in the interest of giving an up-to-date account of where we have come from and where we are now – to help consider how to improve services for children and families for the future.

---

[26] https://www.legislation.gov.uk/ukpga/2002/38/notes/division/2

[27] *Journal of Children's Services,* Volume 5, Issue 2, June 2010, and Volume 5, Issue, 3 September 2010

Public and Private Law

Writing in the journal *Child and Family Law Quarterly* in 2013,[28] Andrew Bainham QC summarises the scope of his thought-provoking paper as follows:

> Legal disputes concerning children are divided conceptually into private or public law. This binary classification disguises the reality that many such cases are hybrid, containing elements of both. The high incidence of these cases requires consistency in the fundamental principles which govern private and public law. It is argued in this paper that the welfare principle now dominates all children proceedings to the extent that the public law threshold, thought to be critical to state intervention, is often marginalised. Welfare also now governs adoption law, notwithstanding that adoption is today primarily a child-protection mechanism.
>
> The involvement of local authorities in private law proceedings invites a reappraisal of the courts' powers; the differential treatment of relatives in the private and public law is questionable; the basis for compulsory state intervention at the interim stage of care proceedings is arguably insufficiently rigorous; and the heavy reliance by the state on the relatively nebulous concepts of neglect and emotional harm calls into question the adequacy of the statutory threshold. It is finally questionable why the concept of the 'good enough' parent applies in the public but not in the private law, yet the state removes children from parents to alternative carers under both.

End of an Era

Rupert Hughes CBE died on 15 August 2015. His funeral took place in London on 26 August. I was asked speak about his professional work and was able to consult widely with former colleagues. My address ended on a more personal but strongly held note:

> *Finally, perhaps two examples of tributes to Rupert sum up what so many of us feel. 'It seems like the end of an era of working for better child care, over which Rupert presided with great leadership and integrity' and 'I am so shocked and upset. He was everything you said and a wonderful friend. He's been an incredibly important person in my life.'*

An obituary was published in The Guardian on 26 August.[29] Later that autumn a celebratory event took place in central London attended by his many friends and former colleagues. A panel of speakers chaired by Wendy Rose included Lady Justice Hale and the former Secretary of State

[28] CFLQ_CFLQ_2013_2_Articles_2_sys.pdf (fourteen.co.uk)

[29] Rupert Hughes obituary | Society | The Guardian

for Health, Virginia Bottomley. With the family's agreement, the following spring a former colleague and friend and I scattered Rupert's ashes on top of Lochnagar (1,155m) in the Cairngorms National Park. This was a mountain he had climbed many times over the years, as had I. We did so together in 2014 to celebrate his 80th birthday.

Book and Film

Unusually, perhaps even uniquely for any post-Second World War parliamentary legislation, the Children Act 1989 features in the acclaimed 2014 novel The Children Act by Ian McEwan[30] and in the 2017 film adaptation. The Guardian reviews of both book and film are referenced in the footnotes.[31]

---

[30] https://www.theguardian.com/books/2014/sep/07/the-children-act-review-ian-mcewan-masterly

[31] https://www.theguardian.com/film/2017/sep/10/the-children-act-review-emma-thompson-ian-mcewan-toronto-film-festival-tiff#:~:text=The%20Children%20Act%20is%20concerned,and%20vulnerable%2C%20carries%20the%20picture.

4

The Future of Welfare Support Services

This chapter outlines the main steps after the 1997 general election that led up to the 1998 consultation paper about the future provision of welfare support services to the family courts and continues by outlining what the consultation paper discussed.

Summary Timeline

My summary of the period from June 1997 to July 1998 includes:[1]

> The Comprehensive Spending Review announced by the Chief Secretary of the Treasury in June 1997 (just after the Election) afforded just the opportunity we had been waiting for to discuss with the Home Office and the Lord Chancellor's Department the idea of bringing together the Galro services; family court welfare and the children's work of the Official Solicitor's Department. The group met at the LCD – Brenda Griffiths-Williams, Joan Bonelle, Peter Harris (the Official Solicitor) and myself. We were quickly able to draft a paper of about 30 paragraphs and submit it to ministers. They agreed early in 1998 that we should proceed to work up a consultation paper. This was announced in Parliament in February. We had our first advisory group meeting in March, having selected the members well in advance and pencilled in dates. Our second meeting was in April and our third in May. The consultation paper ... was published at the end of July.

Consultation Paper

The consultation paper's announced terms of reference were:

> To identify the range of welfare services currently provided by the Probation Service, the Guardian Ad Litem and Reporting Officer Service and the children's work of the Official Solicitor's Department and other agencies in family proceedings, and to consider the scope for improvements to the effectiveness of their work through the creation of a new unified service. To make proposals on the structure of a new service; to provide preliminary analysis of the estimated costs and benefits as a basis for public consultation; and to consider the implications for any new structure of the Government's plans to establish a Wales Assembly.

---

[1] Op. cit. 6

The consultation paper 'Support Services in Family Proceedings: Future Organisation of Court Welfare Services'[2] was commissioned by ministers and published by the Department of Health in conjunction with the Lord Chancellor's Department, the Home Office and the Welsh Office. Ministers wanted practitioners and other service-users to be involved, and the assistance and advice of a number of organisations and individuals is gratefully acknowledged. However, it is also stressed that responsibility for the contents of the consultation paper lies with officials and 'it follows that the views expressed in the paper should not be taken in all instances as having the unanimous and unreserved support of all working group members'.

Membership

The working group was made up from members of the judiciary; the Local Government Association; The Law Society; the Association of Directors of Social Services (ADSS); HM Inspectorate of Probation; the Central Probation Council; the Association of Chief Officers of Probation; the National Association of Guardians Ad Litem and Reporting Officers (Nagalro); and the Association of Guardians Ad Litem and Reporting Officer's panel managers. However, there was criticism from some quarters that the working group should have included a much wider range of stakeholders.

Views Sought

The consultation paper only set out the current arrangements of welfare support service provision across England and Wales, as in Scotland and Northern Ireland different legal provisions cover family proceedings and welfare services to courts. The four areas where views of consultees were particularly sought were the proposals for a new unified service; overall aims and organisational structure; management, administration, staffing and accountability; and representation of children in proceedings. The consultation paper posed 22 questions and invited responses by 13 November 1998.

---

[2] Department of Health Publications, PO Box 410, Wetherby, LS237LN, ref. LASSL (1998)11

Numbers

Family Court Welfare Services

The consultation paper explains that expenditure on family court welfare work accounts for less than 10% of the total Probation Service cash limit and less than 10% of staff resources, although the percentages vary significantly from probation area to area. It is not a 'stand-alone' service, and although in some cases family court welfare (FCW) staff occupy separate buildings, others share premises and support personnel with staff engaged in criminal justice work.

In 1998 there were nearly 700 court welfare officers, of whom just over 70 were designated as senior court welfare officers. Administrative support and clerical staff involved in FCW were estimated as about 280 full-time equivalents. FCW prepared about 36,100 welfare reports to courts per year in England and Wales in 1997 and slightly more, 36,800, the previous year. The volume of mediation cases undertaken had reduced steadily, with 13,800 in 1995 and about 8,300 in 1997. Additionally, the Probation Service has partnership arrangements in the order of £1m in support of FCW work, such as contact centres and out-of-court mediation.

The Official Solicitor

The consultation paper explains that the role of the Official Solicitor in child-related proceedings is to act as the child's solicitor. It is also to give the child or incapacitated parent a voice in the proceedings by making such submissions to the court, having regard to the expressed wishes and views of the child 'as he thinks consistent with the child or adult's welfare and best interests'.

As of March 1997, there were 5,201 cases in hand, of which 1,336 (26%) were children litigation and 226 (4%) were child abductions. 'The Office is staffed by civil servants who may have professional legal qualifications or/and some training in aspects of social work, such as child protection, child development and the interviewing of children. Family cases are undertaken by four lawyers (full-time equivalents) and 57 other staff.' The consultation paper only addresses the future arrangements for the children's welfare side of the Official Solicitor's responsibilities.

The Galro Service

The overall picture of Galro service provision described in the consultation paper was made up in the following ways. The administrative vehicle for the delivery of the Galro service was the panel of Galros assisted by the largely advisory functions of the panel committee. Both operated within the statutory framework of the 1991 panel regulations, as amended. As already mentioned, there were 54 panels in England and five in Wales. Local authorities, if they so chose, could contract out the day-to-day administration of the Galro service to a voluntary organisation or other body. At that time three panels in England were contracted out, as were two in Wales. All were run by different and highly regarded voluntary child care organisations.

As of March 1998, there were an estimated 1,011 guardian 'memberships' in England and 58 in Wales. Of this total of 1,069, 149 (14%) were local authority employees; 5 were probation officer members whose duties were restricted to adoption cases; and 72 were employees of voluntary child care or other organisations. The remainder were self-employed and total 843 (79%). Some self-employed Galros were members of more than one panel, membership of two or three being quite common. For this reason, although the total number of memberships was known, the number of individual guardians that this covered was not; nor was it possible to give an accurate figure for the number of Galro full-time equivalents.

There were about 70 persons designated as panel management staff in England and Wales, of whom 26 were full-time and the remainder part-time. Ninety-two persons were designated as clerical and administrative posts, of whom 44 were full-time and the remainder part-time.

Guardians ad litem and reporting officers in England were appointed in around 13,300 proceedings annually. Of these, about 4,400 (33%) related to adoption proceedings, and the remainder were applications under the Children Act 1989. In Wales there were around 830 proceedings annually, with similar proportions to England relating to adoption and Children Act matters. Around 61% of adoption cases involved a reporting officer, and the remaining adoption applications (39%) required a guardian ad litem.

Local Authority Social Services Departments

These departments also provided information in family proceedings and contributed towards service provision in the following ways:

- the preparation of welfare reports under section 7 of the Children Act 1989 in private law applications, but usually where the social services department has some relevant involvement with the family
- presenting information on child and family welfare issues as applicants (or respondents) in public law proceedings, principally under section 31 (care/child protection) but also relating to other orders that may be sought under the Children Act 1989
- where child protection concerns are raised in the course of private proceedings, and under section 37 the court directs the local authority to undertake an investigation
- preparation of Schedule 2 reports in adoption-related proceedings
- some partnership funding with voluntary organisations

The consultation paper did not discuss at length the role of local authorities described above and therefore made no recommendations about these functions. The Criminal Justice and Court Services Act 2000, which later established Cafcass, made no significant changes to the Children Act 1989.

Welfare Support Services Costs

Chapter 5 of the consultation paper addressed current welfare support service costs, legal representation costs, future funding and transitional costs. Each had serious presentational weaknesses, which included reliance on partial historic data collections and broad estimates, as well as definitional variations and unknown future predictions.

Against such an unpromising background and hedged by many caveats, the headline expenditures offered for family court welfare, Galro and Official Solicitor (Children) for 1997/98 were (in £ thousands) £34,731, £26,193 and £5,572 respectively, which totalled £66.496 million. Separate representation costs in public law cases for guardians (i.e. not including all parties) over a recent 12-month period was estimated at £318,000.

Transitional and Future Service Costs

Ten factors were outlined at paragraph 5.11 as examples affecting the size of transitional costs that might have been incurred over a period of possibly between 18 and 24 months, the crucial feature being that they were all additional to current service costs. The 10 factors were:

> Terms of reference given to the transitional operation; expected duration of transitional period; whether the proposed organisation is required to take on new responsibilities over and above current ones; scale of purchasing and procurement of premises and equipment for the transitional period and for the initial and medium-term requirements of the organisation; relocation costs; staffing costs for any implementation team; other staffing issues, such as a preservation of accrued rights and pension rights; development of new national standards; specialist advice and consultancy; training for the new arrangements.

On future service costs, the consultation paper stated that 'these can only be estimated in the context of possible responsibilities of the new service' (i.e. its structure, remit and workload) and added that 'were these to be broadly similar to current arrangements, estimated costs may be around £66.5 million per year at current prices'.

Analysis

No detailed analysis of the 300 responses received to the consultation paper appears to have survived for inclusion in this book, so it is now not possible to say with certainty if or how any specific concerns were directly taken into account in preparing the enabling legislation, or by the project implementation team or, later still, by Cafcass.

The Acronym

The final 'S' for 'support' was added to the acronym CAFCAS, mainly due to strong arguments in favour advanced by the senior family judiciary during the consultation paper meetings. In July 1999 ministers announced that when legislation allowed, a new unified service would be established across England and Wales; the Lord Chancellor would take the lead responsibility and set up an implementation team; and the new body would be a non-departmental public body (NDPB). This term is discussed in more detail in the next chapter.

Pre- and Post-consultation Concerns

Although the principle of a unified service seemed to have widespread support, there were a number of concerns, many of which were not directly addressed by the bill and continued to be the subject of debate for many years after Cafcass was established. These included fears of a top heavy, over-managed structure and inadequate funding.

For example, soon after the review was announced, Judith Timms, then chief executive of the National Youth Advocacy Service, whose main concern was to establish a freestanding right of children and young people to be consulted and to have a representative speak for them in court, wrote[3] about the context in which the review was announced:

> The first responsibility of any unified service will be to promote the welfare of the children involved in a variety of proceedings across the family jurisdiction, and this cannot be done without protecting the rights of children within those proceedings. In this context it would have been more encouraging if the review had been announced within the framework of the Government's commitment to full implementation of the UN Convention on the Rights of the Child rather than as part of the comprehensive spending review.

Recollections

David Walton, as Staffordshire's chief probation officer from 1990, recalls:

> *I was proud of our FCWS. It developed a very clear professional focus on dispute-resolution/agreement-seeking between parents for the purpose of securing the best future care arrangements for the children. I felt somewhat conflicted about the handover to CAFCASS. On the one hand … we had developed good practices for FCW and did not want to lose it but … the increasingly explicit criminal justice focus to the core work of probation, it was a little incongruous for us to retain statutory responsibilities in the civil courts.*

He further comments:

> *It was perhaps an irony that, although FCW constituted only about 10% of our workload, there was a tendency for the majority of the few complaints received … from service users to be from aggrieved parents, normally fathers, about FCW – not surprisingly these were often quite tense scenarios reflecting the strife in family relationships.*

In his view 'the incisive investigation, and response to such complaints, could often be an important part of bringing the feuding parties to terms with their situation and the future'.

Family court welfare seems to have been of a secondary order of importance in Home Office priorities, and also perhaps at local probation

[3] 'Child Welfare Services', Judith Timms, Family Law, April 1998

committee and chief probation officer levels. John Walters, who was chief probation officer for part of London from 1984 to 2001, recalls:

> *Although the professional head of the family court welfare service, I always felt a dissonance with my principal role as chief officer of an offender correctional service ... I was conscious of redefining the principal role of the service away from being a social work advisory service to the courts ... Family court welfare had no real connection with a correctional service, and it was not possible to define a statement of purpose which covered two entirely different activities ... Probation officers assigned to family court welfare work ... measured their effectiveness by a focus on mediation ... I supported this ... because it seemed to be an effective way of reducing harmful family conflict ... I was not at the time aware of any steps we took to measure the effectiveness of this approach or the extent to which it penetrated family court welfare practice ... we were altogether less rigorous in directing and measuring family court welfare practice than we were with our offender correctional work ... looking at our corporate plan for 2000/2001 I have to conclude that our family court welfare work was very lightly directed. I was frankly pleased that it was passed over to CAFCASS.*

Mary Anne McFarlane, a former chief probation officer in the South West of England, recalls her experiences of family court welfare in the mid- to late 1970s:

> *I thought it was a good approach to child welfare, but the only real aggression she ever experienced was with fathers. Later when she was lead for the Bill team in 1999–2000 in liaison with the Lord Chancellor's office in relation to the CAFCASS clauses she thought the new safeguarding provisions were helpful but the leadership of the new service was highly problematic and did not get it off to a good start.*

Other Perspectives

Susan Cooper recalls enjoying all aspects of the guardian role:

> *And promoting the interests of the child, as independent investigator, as report writer, as expert witness ... the very large patch I covered included both urban poverty and lovely countryside ... and a variety of courts, from the High Court to tiny magistrates' courts. Working with the local authority SSD was mostly good ... except when they disagreed!*

Susan Cooper also comments:

> *Although we guardians were well aware of the need for an independent organisation from which to operate – and indeed campaigned for it – there*

was a real risk that the professional autonomy which we enjoyed, would transfer to the new agency.

Working as the Birmingham Galro panel manager from 1999 to 2001, Azora Hurd considers that the service, while demanding, was one of the most important areas of social work practice to help safeguard and protect vulnerable children. She recalls that the panel was a very busy one that:

Required managing the largest unitary local authority in Europe at the time ... My role ... was a challenging one ... mainly due to the high number of cases before the courts, the allocation of budget and the shortage of guardians practising within the region ... but there was a good relationship between the local authority and the district judge, who ensured that the service was maintained to a high standard. Guardians were held to account for their assessments and judgements as they were required to be regularly assessed.

Richard White was a member of the Children's Panel of solicitors since its inception in about 1984 and was also editor of the Association of Lawyers for Children (ALC) Newsletter. He recalls that:

Solicitors tried to work with specific guardians to ensure better relationships. At some point in the history, it came about that guardians were appointed first and instructed a solicitor of their choosing – a bone of contention, because some solicitors felt they were less likely to get instructions.

He also comments:

Solicitors were appointed first because of the shortage of guardians. That led to questions about the ability of solicitors to take decisions about handling of the case in the absence of a guardian – which at some points could be months.

Susan Cooper worked both as an employed and self-employed guardian in the north and north-east of England between 1984 and 2001. She acted in the High Court in the lead Cleveland child abuse scandal case in 1987.[4] She recalls:

Good and bad memories – the case was both pioneering and exciting, but also vexing, as the judge had made up her mind – and said so – even at the start of the hearing ... The case also raised the question of how guardians would be paid for working in the High Court prior to 1992.

---

[4] The Cleveland Inquiry report was commissioned by the Secretary of State for Social Services in July 1987 and published in 1988. It was led by Dame Elizabeth Butler-Sloss and concluded that most of the diagnoses were incorrect. As a result, 94 of the 121 children were returned to their homes.

And from a different perspective, Anthony Douglas became chair of the Inner and North London Galro panel in about 1996 as part of his wider role of chairing the London Association of Directors of Children's Services (ADCS):

> *I believed in the principles from the start, and I still do ... Our infrastructure was threadbare, with 1.5 panel management posts responsible for over 400 guardians. The most they could do was administer claims and maintain relationships as best they could, especially with some powerful individuals ... we ran an equalisation scheme across the 26 London boroughs involved ... I learnt how you get agreement to changes just by sending invoices to the responsible individual further down the food chain rather than presiding over squabbling ... by certain directors.*

Turning the Page

Efforts in the guardian world increasingly turned to thinking about the future, while at the same time coping with a varied range of current service demands and challenges around the country.

5

Preparing for Cafcass

This chapter highlights some of the activities that were undertaken in preparation for Cafcass once the government had announced how it intended to legislate for a new service. This includes drafting both primary and secondary legislation, the work of an interdepartmental project team and recruitment of a board and senior staff for Cafcass. Some wider organisational issues are also discussed about non-departmental public bodies (NDPBs) and the Lord Chancellor's Department's key operational objectives for Cafcass.

The Legislation

In November 1999 there was a further ministerial announcement that the legislation would be included in the new parliamentary session. The Criminal Justice and Court Services Bill 2000 was led by the Home Office, since most of its provisions concerned the setting up of the National Probation Service. As such, and given typical pressures on parliamentary time and the number of bills that can be successfully managed in a parliamentary session, it was both a convenient and available vehicle to carry the Cafcass-related provisions.[1]

Its successful passage was aided by it having cross-party support, so there was no significant political opposition. It is worth noting that the Children Act 1989 also had cross-party support, albeit led by a Conservative administration. MPs were perhaps also helped by the services of the social policy section of the House of Commons Library, which published a comprehensive research paper about the background to the bill.[2]

[1] Other bills receiving royal assent on 30 November 2000 were the Race Relations (Amendment) Act 2000; Children (Leaving Care) Act 2000; Freedom of Information Act 2000; Countryside and Rights of Way Act 2000; Transport Act 2000; Insolvency Act 2000; Protection of Animals (Amendment) Act 2000; Political Parties, Elections and Referendums Act 2000; Disqualifications Act 2000; Sexual Offences (Amendment) Act 2000.

[2] Criminal Justice and Court Service Bill: Children and Family Court Advisory and Support Service, Disqualification from Working with Children, and Truancy (Bill 91 of 1999–2000) (parliament.uk)

Comments in Parliament

In March 2000 the bill was published and started its parliamentary stages, eventually receiving royal assent on Thursday, 30 November 2000. Debating the bill on 28 March 2000, the then Secretary of State for the Home Department, Mr Jack Straw, said:[3]

> *The restructuring of the probation service provides a timely opportunity to create a new service that focuses on the needs of children and families going through the court system, principally in respect of civil proceedings ... The bill will create a single service to replace the [named former services].*

He continued:

> *CAFCASS ... will be responsible for safeguarding the welfare of children before courts dealing with family court proceedings. Its aim will be to put children first and to offer a fast, flexible and consistent service. The probation service will then be able to concentrate on its main purpose of law enforcement.*

Sir Nicholas Lyell, the former Attorney General from 1992 to 1997, offered some important observations in saying:[4]

> *A portion of the bill deals with court welfare officers and guardians ad litem and the transfer of responsibility from the Home Office to the Lord Chancellor's Department. It has not taken up a great deal of time during the debate. However, it is an extraordinarily difficult matter for any government. It is not party political.*

He stressed:

> *There is quite a difference in culture at present between court welfare officers and guardians ad litem. Court welfare officers deal with day-to-day work for particular courts and undertake valuable work. They are full-time employees. Guardians ad litem are somewhat differently trained. They are estimable people who largely work freelance.*

He then warned:

> *It is important that the Lord Chancellor's Department should be sensitive in moulding the two services together. It should be realised that the Home Office was probably not wholly altruistic in passing responsibility to the Lord Chancellor's Department in these often extremely contentious matters ... The whole issue of child care when dealt with in the courts, and of marriage*

---

[3] https://hansard.parliament.uk/commons/2000-03-28/debates/cebd5a12-e2ff-4ce8-b2e2-ec18051b3e63/CriminalJusticeAndCourtServicesBill

[4] Ibid. Cols 256 and 257

breakdown, which is so often the background, is hugely contentious and is known to lead to many complaints.

His final remarks offer a further note of caution:

The Home Office is a rather large department compared with the Lord Chancellor's Department. The Lord Chancellor may be pleased to be enlarging his empire, but let him ensure that the formidable reputation on which he relies is effective in the courts as the Chancellor of the Exchequer. Otherwise, he will not have the budget to do the job properly. I wish him well, not only for his sake but for that of those in the service, who will depend on his success if they are to be able to do a very difficult job effectively.

Demands and Slips

I wrote:[5]

The voracious appetite of the bill team, often demanding at short notice information about the Galro service and its history. I also remember that the bill was nearly lost on 30 November due to disagreement about obscure probation estate ownership matters ... and that the Cafcass clauses received general support but attempts to shorten or find an alternative acronym were unsuccessful.

Later the Act's commencement date was announced for 1 April 2001.[6] The Home Office was responsible for arranging publication of the Act with The Stationery Office. I wrote:[7]

I immediately noticed that they had printed the wrong title on the cover and also on the first few pages of the Act, inserting an extra 's' to call it the Criminal Justice and Courts Services Act 2000. I emailed my Home Office colleague asking how such as silly mistake ... could have occurred. I got no answer – but she did copy my email to just about everyone in the Home Office.

Secondary Legislation

There was also the need to amend secondary legislation in 2001, such as four sets of court rules.[8] These set out in detail the powers and duties of Cafcass officers when appointed in both public and private law proceedings. I worked with the LCD lawyer Kathy Hodgson and wrote the guidance that was published in March 2001. I also wrote:[9]

[5] Op. cit. 6

[6] Section 80

[7] Op. cit. 6

[8] The Family Proceedings Courts (Children Act 1989) (Amendment) Rules 2001, https://www.legislation.gov.uk/uksi/2001/818/made?view=plain

[9] Op. cit. 6

> At one stage in January we sat round with the president looking over our drafts. About 10 other judges and a number of LCD and DH officials also attended. The purpose was to ensure that there were no mistakes that might cause legal trouble later. A number of useful suggestions were made. I am sure the rules benefited by having that kind of scrutiny conducted in a cordial atmosphere.

I recall with gratitude the unwavering support I always received from successive presidents of the Family Division and many other senior judiciary around the country:

> *Whatever the problems – and there were many – Sir Stephen would often end the conversations by patting me on the back and commenting, 'Never mind ... it's not as bad as the Arctic convoys!'*

Sir Stephen Brown was president of the Family Division (1988–99) and was succeeded as president by Dame Elizabeth Butler-Sloss (1999–2005). From 1943 to 1946 Sir Stephen served in the Royal Naval Reserves assigned to the Arctic supply convoys. I remained in touch with him for many years about his naval service and links with North West Scotland. I was also a guest at his retirement dinner at Inner Temple.

The Interdepartmental Project Team

The interdepartmental project team operated from 1999 to 2001. I also wrote:[10]

> To start with, the CAFCASS project team was made up of Helen Hartwell, Joan Bonelle, David Lye, Bridget Ogden and Wendy Mason. It is not appropriate at this time to comment in detail on each of them. But it is necessary to say that there was a marked contrast after the project was set up in November 1999 with the relaxed style and approach we achieved from June 1997 onwards. In short, it was felt that there was poor leadership and management, and there was also in one team member outrageously aggressive, intimidating and rude behaviour.

I added:[11]

> In this period I made about 30 to 40 visits around the country talking to the judiciary, family court welfare and the guardian world about the proposals.

[10] Op. cit. 6

[11] Op. cit. 6

> It was thoroughly enjoyable, and wherever I went there was a good quality of debate and some considerable enthusiasm for the project. On a number of these visits, Helen [Hartwell] and I did a 'double act' … and, if needed, this helped with lowering the tension.

David Lye, as project director, addressed guardians in an article for *Seen and Heard*[12] in wholly positive terms, stressing that Cafcass remained on course for launch in April 2001 and that:

> A lot of the basic infrastructure is now coming to completion including:
>
> – terms and conditions for employees to transfer under TUPE[13] and that self-employed would retain their self-employed status;
> – details of all the accommodations likely to transfer to Cafcass;
> – an intention to develop firm proposals on management structures; and
> – launching a project to examine IT with a step-by-step approach.

He went on to stress that 'our approach is one of evolution, not revolution', with the aim of providing as much continuity and stability as possible for people who will work in Cafcass at a time of inevitable uncertainty. Lye repeated his views:

> The opportunities that Cafcass offered to create:
>
> – a child-focused service;
> – a professional service;
> – a better service to children, families and the courts; and
> – an influential, visible and accountable service.

He then enlarged on how the above were going to be realised and opportunities seized. Later he notes:

> As a first step, the process to identify a first-class and diverse Board to lead Cafcass is well in hand. We have received many applications to serve on the Board.

Lye concludes:

> Monthly meetings with NAGALRO now take place and are immensely valuable. Often 'full and frank' in tone, this communication is in the true spirit of Modernising Government,[14] and I am sure that Cafcass will be all the better for it.

---

[12] 'CAFCASS Takes Shape', *Seen and Heard*, Volume 10, Issue 3, 2001

[13] TUPE stands for Transfer of Undertakings Protection of Employment Rights. It is the law that protects employees, and their benefits, when their employment changes hands.

[14] Cm 4310, White Paper presented to Parliament, March 1999

https://ntouk.files.wordpress.com/2015/06/modgov.pdf

Susan Cooper recalls the pre-Cafcass meetings at the Department of Health, when she was the NAGALRO chair:

> *They were dominated by two men in suits from the Probation Service … how dare they! … and the independent guardians whom I was representing were mostly worried about retaining their jobs under comparable conditions. There was an irony in accepting the need for an independent agency, and the integration of the three core services, while at the same time we regarded the juggernaut that was to be CAFCASS with some apprehension.*

Recruitment

Pending royal assent, Cafcass' first chairman of the board was appointed in October 2000, and in November 2000, 10 members of the board were also appointed, although their details were not announced publicly until early 2001. The Act made further provisions[15] for regulations,[16] which contained detailed stipulations. These included that:

> When appointing Board members, the Lord Chancellor shall have regard to the desirability of ensuring that the Service includes persons with expertise in or knowledge of:
>
> (a) management;
> (b) business and finance;
> (c) social conditions relating to children and families; and
> (d) the work of the courts.

An additional power allowed the service to co-opt no more than five persons to the board to provide expertise. However, in the light of later events concerning the board, which are discussed below, it was necessary to update these regulations in 2005, both to address certain difficulties and to take into account the impact of Welsh devolution on Cafcass, which became a non-departmental public body for England alone.

In November 2000, 10 regional manager posts and 10 business unit manager posts were advertised, and in December 2000 the chief executive was appointed. By January 2001, the head of finance, head of human resources and head of legal services had also been appointed. A press notice[17] issued on 15 February 2001 states:

---

15 Section 11 and schedule 2

16 Children and Family Court Advisory and Support Service (Membership, Committee and Procedure) Regulations 2000 (SI 2000/3374)

17 wired-gov.net/wg/wg-news-1.nsf/54e6de9e0c383719802572b9005141ed/ef819c203b3b27048 02572ab004b3c86?OpenDocument

> The Lord Chancellor, Lord Irvine, has appointed the following to the Board of the new Children and Family Court Advisory and Support Service (CAFCASS) when it is established on 1 April 2001. His Honour Judge Nigel Fricker QC, Peter Hargrave, Leonie Jordan, Angela M. Killick, Anne Morgan OBE JP, Pip O'Byrne, Nalini Varma, Mike Walker, Nedine Watson-Cutts, Judy Weleminsky.

It continued:

> The appointment of the chairman, Anthony Hewson, previously chairman of Scope, was announced on 10 November 2000. The Chief Executive, Diane Shepherd, has appointed Charles Prest as Director of Legal Services.[18] Charles is currently a partner in Lee and Priestley Solicitors, Leeds.

The press notice also gave summary details of the professiona backgrounds of board appointees, which presumably aimed to reflect th requirements of the regulations (a) to (d) quoted above. Details of Cafcass first board membership are set out in Appendix One.

Recruitment Process

Other details and questions about the Lord Chancellor and boar recruitment processes – including co-options – remain unanswered. Fo example, who drew up the shortlisted applicants; who sat on th interview panels; how many applicants and from what backgrounds wer turned down; and how was diversity addressed? What is available is se out in the later government's upbeat 2003 response to the select committe report and its critical comments:

> The Board was recruited following a fulsome search and rigorous assessment process, conducted along Nolan principles and within the Commissioner for Public Appointments Guide of Best Practice. Its current membership includes individuals from diverse backgrounds with a wealth of different experience. Many have worked in fields which give them experience – often at senior level – in providing services to children and other in-need groups, alongside experience of managing organizations and some have specific experience of the sphere in which CAFCASS operates.

The Nolan principles published in government guidance in May 199 apply to anyone who works as a public office holder and are (1) selflessness, (2) integrity, (3) objectivity, (4) accountability, (5) openness (6) honesty and (7) leadership.

[18] Charles Prest resigned as Cafcass' Director of Legal Services as of 1 January 2005.

Wider Context

The importance of placing the new service in a wider context was stressed by His Honour Judge Nigel Fricker.[19] His article, written in late 1999, explained that he believed that the way the new service was set up and developed needed to be enlightened by a comprehensive strategy for processing child welfare issues and family dispute resolution:

> CAFCAS should take on the existing child welfare responsibilities of family court welfare, guardian ad litem and reporting officer, and Official Solicitor services. However, my vision is that the overarching concept for CAFCAS should be based on the notion that in the vast majority of child welfare problems and parental disputes judicial decision should be the last resort.

Non-departmental Public Bodies

As Cafcass was established as a non-departmental public body (NDPB), some further explanation of this term is offered. Non-departmental public bodies are said typically to operate at 'arm's length' from government, but that concept does not mean the new organisation is cast adrift. Cafcass was set up to be accountable through its chairman and board to the Lord Chancellor for ensuring that its policies were compatible with those of the Lord Chancellor. In turn, the Lord Chancellor was accountable to Parliament for Cafcass' activities and performance. The information about the statutory and financial framework between the Lord Chancellor and Cafcass was set out in an agreed framework document comprising a management statement and financial memorandum. This NDPB would also be separate from other services to families and parties to the court proceedings.

The preamble to the more recent 32-page framework document dated 2014[20] states:

> This framework document has been drawn up by Cafcass in consultation with the Department and sets out the broad framework within which Cafcass will operate. The document does not convey any legal powers or responsibilities. It is signed and dated by the Department and Cafcass. Copies of the document and any subsequent amendments have been placed in the Libraries of both Houses of Parliament and made available to members of the public on the Cafcass website.

---

[19] 'The New Children and Family Courts Advisory Service', His Honour Judge Nigel Fricker QC, Family Law, February 2000

[20] https://www.cafcass.gov.uk/sites/default/files/migrated/legislation-and-framework-Cafcass-Framework-document.pdf

Key Operational Objectives

In addition to the framework document, the Lord Chancellor set Cafcass six key operational objectives (KOOs). These were:

1. Represent, safeguard and promote the welfare of children involved in family court proceedings
2. Improve the services offered to the family courts.
3. To improve the efficiency and effectiveness of the services offered through increased value for money.
4. To improve the services offered to families and other key stakeholders.
5. To develop the skills of staff.
6. Cafcass should play a full role in delivering the wider government agenda of improvements in service.

Each key objective includes additional explanatory text.[21] Taken together, they illustrate the wide demands and high expectations placed on Cafcass, notwithstanding the complexities of bringing together the 140 existing service providers across the whole of England and Wales[22] and also ensuring continuing service delivery to children, families and courts during the transitional period.

Richard White notes[23] in respect of the first framework document that 'it has become clearer just how much control this document gives the Lord Chancellor's Department (LCD). Although the public position is that decisions are a matter for the board, it is obvious that Cafcass was not allowed to do anything without sanction from the LCD.' And he further argues that it would be wrong to call the framework document 'agreed', as it was imposed on Cafcass without discussion shortly before implementation on 1 April 2001.

Change Management

Having agreed in early 2001 to contribute a chapter to this book,[24] I unwisely shared my draft with a new senior manager at the Department

[21] https://publications.parliament.uk/pa/cm200203/cmselect/cmlcd/614/614w25.htm at paragraph 2.3

[22] It was not until April 2005 that responsibility for the functions of Cafcass in Wales, known as CAFCASS Cymru, was devolved to the National Assembly for Wales.

[23] New Law Journal, 30 November 2001

[24] 'Chapter 11 – The Way Forward; CAFCASS and the Future for the Representation of Children in Family Proceeding' Poyser, Arran, *Hearing the Voice of the Child*, edited by Maria Ruegger, Russell House Publishing, 2001

of Health. He decided he had to read and approve not only my chapter but also the proposed text for the preceding 10 chapters.

> A sharp exchange of views ensued. I was allowed to proceed when I offered a new opening sentence to my Introduction stating '*The views expressed in this chapter are those of the writer and not necessarily those of the Department of Health or the Lord Chancellor's Department*'. He did not read the rest of the book.

I suggested that not only was preparing for any organisational change complex, but also there were special factors influencing how Cafcass should be established. These include:

- moving about 2,000 staff across England and Wales into Cafcass within the 17-month period from the announcement that there would be legislation to the date the service was due to commence
- securing transfer budgets from current services to Cafcass and start-up funding to cover the implementation project and investment in IT
- managing primary and secondary legislation
- ensuring minimum disruption of services to children, families and courts
- ensuring family court welfare service changes were coordinated with the parallel reorganisation within the same timescale and under the same legislation establishing the National Probation Service
- ensuring wide consultation and involvement of all staff in the change process and also consulting fully with the courts and legal professions and users of the service
- consulting widely with those contracted voluntary organisations providing mediation and guardian panel services
- harmonising current salaries and self-employment issues

I also emphasised the need to devolve authority, responsibility and decision-making vested with the current service providers and the four government departmental sponsors to the project team, board chair, board members, chief executive and senior managers. However, the issue around the self-employed guardians was a major difficulty.

Self-employment

Writing in 2001,[25] I also said:

> What has completely thrown everyone off course is the issue of self-employment in the eyes of the Inland Revenue Service. They decided in the autumn of 2000 that by 1 April 2001, new self-employment contracts for about 750 former self-employed guardians would need to be drawn up. This bombshell has had profound knock-on effects. It was assumed by those planning Cafcass that over time (that is, in two to three years after April 2001) new contracts for both self-employed and employed would need to be drawn up. This is because of the wide variations in inherited pay and conditions for those who have joined Cafcass. All this needed 'harmonisation' – a complex issue, as this is in effect not the merger of three organisations; rather, it is one of bringing together over 120 local services, each with different arrangements for pay and related matters ... Pay has completely dominated the agenda for the crucial period of months (already perilously short) between royal assent ... and the start of the service.

Azora Hurd, in her role as Birmingham Galro panel manager, also played a part between November 2000 and April 2001 with the many transitional arrangements that were being made to help establish Cafcass.

> *I recall being involved in some of the national policy-making steering groups so that the new organisation had them in place upon inception of CAFCASS ... I worked very closely with fellow panel managers to provide our perspective in managing the service so that this tacit knowledge was not lost.*

Training and Continuous Professional Development

I also stressed[26] that the main principle that Cafcass is committed to support is to ensure that whenever its officers are appointed to advise the courts, they have the training, skills and experience relevant to those proceedings and that the management and administration within Cafcass serve to support this aim. I argued that Cafcass activities are not seen as suitable for new social work graduates; instead, the organisation is likely to need to rely on those who are both well qualified and experienced.

In pointing out that there is no social work training at either a basic level or an advanced level, such as a master's degree that focuses on Cafcass alone, I concluded by highlighting the need to invest in the continuous professional development of all Cafcass staff and that such an approach requires both funding and a change of culture. The cultural

[25] Op. cit. 6

[26] Ibid.

change is to establish Cafcass as a 'learning agency' that has been defined as 'an organisation that demonstrably takes an integrated and coordinated approach to training and related issues, such as practice and evidence-based research, appraisal and continuing development of all staff'.

Lord Chancellor's Departmental Report

In introducing his departmental report in March 2001,[27] the Lord Chancellor described in more general and upbeat terms the new organisation:

> Stronger families and the protection of children's rights contribute to social cohesion and fairness in society ... a new agency, will combine the family court welfare functions ... Its purpose is to provide a fast, flexible and consistent service which has a clear focus on the interests of children ...
>
> One of [its] main roles will be to represent the voice of the child in court proceedings ... Bringing these services together means the Department can better serve the interests of children in court and provide modern, common-sense arrangements focused on the needs of children and families.

And later, the same report states:[28]

> Much work was carried out to create the new body and to ensure a smooth transition to the new system. It was ready and able to take over this work on 1 April as planned. The new unified service will bring improvements in the services offered to children, families and the courts and will provide these services more flexibly and efficiently. In doing so, it will fulfil its paramount objective of safeguarding and promoting the welfare of children. The work of CAFCASS and its officers will be subject to independent inspection by HM Magistrates' Courts Service Inspectorate.

However, as is discussed later in Chapter 7, the Lord Chancellor's claim that 'it was ready and able to take over this work' and the aspiration to ensure 'a smooth transition to the new system' both fell short by a considerable margin in the eyes of many and was roundly criticised in the 2003 select committee's inquiry about Cafcass.[29]

---

[27] Lord Chancellor's Department departmental report, March 2001

[28] Ibid. page 46

[29] Op. cit. 120

Incorrect Guidance

The *Working Together* government guidance published in July 2018, refers to the Children Act 1989 rather than the Criminal Justice and Court Services Act 2000, stating:[30]

> 52. The responsibility of the Children and Family Court Advisory and Support Service (Cafcass), as set out in the Children Act 1989, is to safeguard and promote the welfare of individual children who are the subject of family court proceedings. This is through the provision of independent social work advice to the court.

I drew this information to the attention of DfE officials in January 2020. Their response included:

> Thank you for your email of 22 January about the Working Together to Safeguard Children (2018) guidance. We have noted the issue you have raised regarding the responsibility of the Children and Family Court Advisory and Support Service (Cafcass) as set out in legislation and will include it for consideration as part of the next review and update of the guidance. Thank you for raising this issue.

It appears that no review and update have yet taken place.

Northern Ireland, Ireland and Scotland

In Northern Ireland, the Children Act Order[31] made much of the Children Act 1989 applicable there in the mid-1990s. They set up the Galro service based on the English 1991 panel regulations and as one of the Health and Social Care Board's responsibilities rather than administered separately. Their first panel manager joined in a number of the events I organised, including panel management training and annual Galro conferences.

There was no formal consultation between Belfast and London about, for example, our experience and lessons learnt in applying the 1991 regulations. These broadly continued the 1984 arrangements whereby local authorities in England and Wales were responsible for the Galro service, although they were the parties bringing most public law proceedings. Despite ameliorating features that tried to strengthen

---

[30] *Working Together to Safeguard Children: A guide to inter-agency working to safeguard and promote the welfare of children*, page 72

https://assets.publishing.service.gov.uk/media/5fd0a8e78fa8f54d5d6555f9/Working_together_to_safeguard_children_inter_agency_guidance.pdf

[31] The Children (Northern Ireland) Order 1995 (legislation.gov.uk)

perceptions of independence, this system, understandably for some, called into question its actual operational independence.

The Irish NSPCC, based in Dublin, was interested in setting up a guardian service. Anna Faulkner, as panel manager from the Inner and North London panel, and I were invited to Dublin to discuss their ideas. It was apparent that their different legal framework made the concept of a guardian and solicitor acting 'in tandem' for the child very difficult, and no more was heard about it in London.

The Nuffield Foundation funded a study[32] on comparative Anglo-Irish child-related divorce legislation that also provides an invaluable wider historical context. An earlier version of this report was prepared for successful residential symposium held in May 2002 at Dartington Hall, Devon, which I attended with many others from a wide range of professional backgrounds.

Chapter 11 of the Report on the Accounts of the Public Service 2015[33] provides a detailed account of guardian-related issues in Ireland (including some comparisons with England, Wales and Scotland) provided by Tulsa, which is a statutory organisation established in 2014 under the Children and Family Agency Act 2013.

Arrangements for dealing with a range of children and family matters in Scotland, which like Ireland has an entirely different history and legal system, are not covered in this book. Key milestones were the Kilbrandon Report in 1964[34] and the Social Work (Scotland) Act 1968.[35] Later reviews followed and are pending.

---

[32] *The Voice of the Child in Private Family Law Proceedings*, Murch, M. and Keehan, G., Family Law, 2003

[33] https://assets.gov.ie/37358/c31b8d3e03d049a390a1900fa37856ea.pdf

[34] https://www.gov.scot/binaries/content/documents/govscot/publications/independent-report/2003/10/kilbrandon-report/documents/0023863-pdf/0023863-pdf/govscot%3Adocument/0023863.pdf

[35] https://www.legislation.gov.uk/ukpga/1968/49/contents/enacted

6

Cafcass' First Years

This chapter examines some of the difficulties Cafcass had to address during its first operational years, including a board member resignation and the loss of key senior management appointees. The board's meetings are also discussed alongside media attention and levels of funding. Details about an important judicial review are also covered.

Vesting Day

Cafcass' vesting day on 1 April 2001 arrived, creating the largest social work organisation in the country. But for many it was not a cause for special celebration. There was much that had not been effectively put in place and the range of serious issues needing urgent attention escalated. Even so, across England and Wales many hundreds of open cases continued to be handled by Cafcass' newly titled front-line caseworkers under transitional arrangements covering both public and private law applications already before the courts. Other interagency arrangements, such as business meetings with the courts and other agencies, also continued.

With this date also ended the 114 organisational arrangements that had provided the former welfare support services. These had comprised family court welfare from 47 probation areas in England and seven in Wales; 54 Galro panels in England and five in Wales; and the Official Solicitor's children's branch.

Writing several years later,[1] Michael Griffith-Jones, Nagalro's first chair said, 'By early 2001, however, the omens were poor. The government had allowed too little time for the complex merger of three disparate organisations. Civil servants delegated to set up the machinery knew nothing about any of the services and so instructed expensive consultants, who produced glossy but often meaningless documents. Vesting day for Cafcass was set, without a hint of irony, as 1 April 2001.'

---

[1] The Guardian Service: A Longitudinal Perspective on the Representation of Children's Welfare in Public Law Proceedings, Griffith-Jones, M., *Seen and Heard,* Volume 16, December 2006

Media Attention About Cafcass

The Guardian's headline on Monday, 2 April 2001 was 'New Start for Welfare of Children in Court'[2] and began:

> The new children and family court welfare service in England and Wales begins its first working day today amid growing controversy … Even before the launch of Cafcass … the complexities of creating a unified body to work in the best interests of the child were already becoming apparent. The challenge of combining … functions that were formerly provided by the three services into one integrated system means the embryonic service has been experiencing some uncomfortable birth pangs.

The Guardian continued by summarising some key issues and viewpoints:

> Guardians ad litem, who represent vulnerable children in public law cases are concerned about the way they will be paid in future. Before Cafcass came into being, the guardians were mostly self-employed, worked for councils and were paid an hourly rate. Under new arrangements, there are plans to pay them under banding systems of fixed fees.
>
> Representatives of Nagalro are arguing that the new arrangements for fixed fees may fundamentally change the way they work and, as a consequence, undermine the vital work they do in representing and safeguarding children. As a result, the association is challenging the proposed pay structure and threatening a judicial review if no acceptable way forward can be found. A six-week moratorium has been agreed to find a solution.
>
> Susan Bindman, chairwoman of Nagalro, said: 'The work that we do is highly complex and demands flexibility. Gathering together all the appropriate information that is required to safeguard a vulnerable child can be extremely time-consuming. Our fear is that under the proposed pay structure many of the fundamental tenets underpinning the work that we do may be lost.'
>
> Anthony Hewson, chairman of Cafcass, says part of the agency's responsibility is to make sure the public purse is being properly used. 'We have a six-week period where we will have to examine the issues. And there are two very different positions. On the one hand we have the Inland Revenue telling us that guardians ad litem cannot be employed under their current terms. But Nagalro does not agree, and the answer is to talk and try to reach an agreement,' he said.
>
> Jim Lawson, a respected senior court welfare officer based in Bristol, said: 'There are a number of potential benefits from an integrated advisory and support service for family courts, not least the fact that there can now be

[2] https://www.theguardian.com/society/2001/apr/02/crime.penal

agreed national standards with practitioners. In the past, family court welfare was formerly part of the probation service and had become extremely marginalised within the service. Guardian panels were administered by the local authority, and that meant the authorities were effectively paying for the guardians.' Mr Lawson sees the challenge for Cafcass as providing a new organisation that will encourage the exchange of skills and contribute to the professional development of all the participants. 'But there may be problems with vested interests if professionals attempt to cling to the past rather than embracing the future,' he warned.

Mr Hewson says delays in the family court system were leading to some children having to wait up to 40 weeks to get into the system: 'In future we will be able to analyse the areas where children are facing unacceptable waiting times and effectively address the problems with a unified approach.' He believes the main task is to listen to the views of children to create a truly child-focused system: 'Over the next 12 months we are going to be asking children what it is that they would like to see in terms of a service. There are many ways we can do this. We have already begun talks with agencies like the NSPCC, and that is crucial to the future.'

The level of media attention during Cafcass' first year was significant, and in the main was highly critical, not only of Cafcass but also of the Lord Chancellor's Department.[3] At times, both Cafcass and the Lord Chancellor's Department appear to have had difficulties in getting their respective points of view heard effectively via the media, including correcting any factual mistakes carried in press stories.

The Board's First Resignation

His Honour Judge Nigel Fricker was among the first board appointees before resigning after a few months due to intractable differences of opinion about the handling of the self-employed guardian dispute. Judge Fricker recalls that episode: 'It was without doubt the most painful time in my professional life.'

Nigel Fricker was another senior family judge with whom I remained in occasional contact up to 2023.

Board Meetings

The minutes of Cafcass board meetings in its first year of operation provide but only a partial picture of frenetic activity by the chairman, other board members and the executive team. The latter are listed

[3] A tragedy of errors | Society | The Guardian | 21 October 2003

technically as 'in attendance' but appear to have been fully involved in discussion. Usually, they include the chief executive, the directors of operations, human resources, finances and legal services.

Even so, these documents tell only some of the story about key concerns and decisions. This is because board meetings also frequently considered papers tabled by the chair, other board members and the chief executive and directors. None of these papers, if they still exist, have been released under Cafcass' freedom of information procedures.

The board established several sub-committees, with membership agreed at its 6 April board meeting. Board minutes were often minimal in style, as was no doubt considered normal in 2001, concentrating on subject headlines, key decisions and identifying the person responsible for carrying out any decided action. What is missing is the 'who said what' of the discussion, as well as, for example, whether views diverged and, if so, whether there was a need for board members to vote to come to a majority decision.

Board meetings were not electronically recorded until some years later. Mention is also made of secretariat shortages hampering the efficient handling of some board activities. Some minutes provided under FOI are headed 'Draft Subject to Revision'.

The board met once in shadow format on 9 March 2001 and also seems to have had a telephone conference on 29 March. There is also a somewhat confused picture of how often the board met. There are minutes for board meetings held on 6 April, 18 April, 18 May, 15 June, 25 June and 25 October 2001. These minutes also make reference to a board meeting date for 28 November and also for dates into 2002. But the minutes of the board meeting held on 25 October state:

> The minutes of 25th July 2001, 5th and 6th September 2001, 19th September 2001 and 8th October 2001 and the summary of a telephone conference on 17th September 2001 were agreed as accurate records of those meetings and signed by the Chairman, subject to the following amendments:

There was also a board 'away day' on 8 and 9 June 2001.

Although the framework document and the Lord Chancellor's Department's six key objectives for Cafcass offer a higher-level strategic overview, what the board minutes suggest is driven far more by a wide range of urgent setting up and transitional practical policy and practice priorities. The extent to which the actions of individual board members were proactive and / or reactive to internal or external pressures can only be a matter of conjecture, without any clearer source of evidence.

With such reservations in mind, great caution is needed in interpreting the following summary example extracts from four sets of board minutes held on 6 April, 18 May, 25 June and 18 October 2001. Even so, the host of serious concerns highlighted from the minutes is palpable. This surely was an organisation under great pressure, if not formally in crisis.

Board Meeting – 6 April 2001

- Resolved: that the minutes of the meeting of the Shadow Board on 9 March be noted. An addendum to those minutes to be prepared for formal approval at the next meeting
- The Chairman reported on the engagements he had undertaken since the telephone conference on 29 March.
- Resolved: that the Chairman's report be noted. In future the Chairman would provide a summary of key issues raised during meetings, when resources permitted.
- The Chief Executive said that future reports would be written. Since taking up her post on 2 April 2001, she had:
  - met all staff at Cafcass headquarters;
  - met Jane Kennedy, Parliamentary Secretary;
  - been involved in media handling;
  - draft answers to five Parliamentary Questions;
  - emailed all Cafcass staff; and
  - met with the trade unions.
- She also reported on the recruitment of Directors ... the Director of Operations would take up post at the end of May; the post of Director of Finance had been verbally accepted. All ten Area Managers had been selected and six had taken up posts. Interim Managers were in post in the other four areas.
- Members of the Board discussed how the Task and Finish Groups might be established and resolved that these be finalised after the Chief Executive's conference with Cafcass managers. The Chairman and Chief Executive to decide which Board Members are members of each group.
- Resolved that the Chairman chair the Finance Committee and that the members are Nigel Fricker, Judy Weleminsky, Leonie Jordan and Mike Walker.
- Resolved that Peter Hargrave chair the Audit Committee and that Anne Morgan, Angela Killick, Nalini Varma and Nedine Watson-Cutts be members.

- The Secretary to the Board explained that Members would be asked to rank the three Members standing for election [of Deputy Chair of the Board] ... Following voting ... resolved that subject to the Lord Chancellor's approval, Anne Morgan be elected Deputy Chair of Cafcass.

Board Meeting – 18 May 2001

The Chairman highlighted some aspects of his tabled Paper. For example:

- He had 'addressed 280 delegates at the Association of Black Probation Officers conference in Manchester. It had been a very positive experience, and there had been real enthusiasm for CAFCASS.'
- On discussion on the interview with The Guardian, Board members suggested that:
  - key messages were needed for media handling;
  - a proactive strategy was required, and feature editors might be more receptive to a good story than reporters.

The Chief Executive reported that:

- the actuarial review of the pension scheme would be started urgently;
- a communications strategy would be presented to the next Board meeting and she had appeared before the Adoption Bill Select Committee ...[4]

The Chief Executive also reported that:

- 'she had attended the first meeting of the Sponsor Unit in the LCD. She had given the Unit a paper on the priorities for the coming months and a draft Business Plan. This was "tabled". She had been unhappy about presenting these to the Sponsor Department before the Board had seen the documents. The Board took a clear view that the documents should in future generally be submitted to the Board before going to the LCD.'

It was also suggested that the Board should receive a presentation on the legal responsibilities as a body corporate.

The Chief Executive also reported that:

- A second conference had taken place to invest in the management team;
- *Panorama* had requested permission to film families, and CAFCASS needed to have a policy on the issue;
- She had had an introductory meeting with the Lord Chancellor, where guardians' contracts was the major issue discussed;
- She had identified the need for an IT Director/Manager;
- She needed the Board's agreement to place an OJEC notice in relation to IT case-management procurement. The Board agreed this should proceed;

---

[4] Referred to in more detail later in this chapter.

- She had met representatives of a number of CAFCASS groups to discuss how, if at all, they might fit within the CAFCASS structure; a meeting with the Unions had taken place, but only discussed guardians. It was suggested that an industrial relations framework was needed;
- There were difficulties with IT and telephones at Newspaper House,[5] and the legal team were giving invaluable advice to all CAFCASS staff, but were under-resourced to provide that service.

Board Meeting – 15 June 2021

As the board minutes for 15 June were not included with other minutes when Cafcass responded on 23 June 2023 to my FOI request, no summary of this meeting is included.

Board Meeting – 27 June 2001

- Resolved that the minutes of the meetings of 18 May 2001 and 15 June 2001 be signed by the Chairman as a true record of the meetings.
- The Chairman said that CAFCASS had still not been supplied with details of the work of all of the 16 advisory groups and task teams that had been established by the Project Team. He had been advised that they would be supplied by early July, although some papers were being archived. The Board agreed that CAFCASS needed to have these papers at the earliest opportunity.
- The Chairman set out the Background to the Situation Report (paper tabled). 'He envisaged submitting the report to Joan MacNaughton[6] and inviting her to the September Board meeting to discuss the issues raised'. Sixteen comments are noted but by unnamed members, including, for example:
  - The document was important to the Board, both for its own protection and to draw a line under events;
  - There was a need to reflect members' unhappiness about the project to establish CAFCASS;
  - The process of establishing a shadow Board and executive was inadequate given the scale of the transfer taking place (e.g. the number of terms and conditions that were transferred);
  - The list of practical work that needed to be completed, produced by the Chief Executive, should be added to the Situation Report, as it provided a very clear injection of reality;
  - The sheer volume of 'unknown' information should be set out;
  - There was an urgent need to get the costings right this year and establish the real cost of providing the service;

[5] Cafcass' first headquarters In London was sited behind Victoria Street.

[6] Lord Chancellor's Department Director General Policy 1999–2001

- The time and energy spent on the guardian issue needed to be highlighted;
- The report needed to be expressed in powerful terms, especially the impact these issues were having on staff;
- The report should be finalised as soon as possible and CAFCASS should then seek help and support from the LCD in moving forward.

These minutes continue:

> It was also suggested that it would be useful for the Board to have a paper setting out the liabilities of the Board, (e.g. responsibilities of a NDPB; the relationship with [the] LCD; collective and individual obligations; decision-making power of the Board; and the consequences of failing to make the right decisions).

And the minutes also state:

> It was agreed that the Chairman would revise the Situation Report, taking into account the members' comments, as well of those of the Executive Team. It would then be sent to the Board members for final comments before being submitted to Joan MacNaughton by 6 July 2001.

The chief executive tabled her report to the board:

> It was agreed that the Inspectorate would be invited to give feedback to the Board from their initial inspection at the September meeting.
> It was agreed that Board members would be invited to attend regional conferences for CAFCASS staff and to establish a formal linking of individual Board Members to each of the regions and to Wales.
> The Chief Executive and Chairman felt that the Board needed to find an alternative means of obtaining general legal advice rather than asking the Director of Legal Services ... The Chief Executive was asked to consider how that might be done ... bring options to the Board if necessary ... and to consider longer term options ... [which might include] ... a presentation to the Board.

As the director of legal services not only had to head the casework formerly dealt with by the Official Solicitor children's branch but also address a wide range of other legal issues that the new NDBP faced, this workload was not sustainable and steps were taken to try to resolve it.[7]

Board Meeting – 18 October 2001

The chief executive's apologies for absence are among those noted. The minutes state that:

---

[7] See earlier footnote 18 in Chapter 5.

> Due to other pressures, the Chairman had not been able to provide a written report. He reported that since the meeting on 25 July 2001 he had:
>
> - Attended an away day with the Chief Executive on 30 and 31 July 2001;
> - Addressed the Oxford Family Mediation centre conference on 26 September 2001;
> - Had a further away day with the Chief Executive on 27 and 28 September 2001;
> - Attended and addressed the President's Conference[8] on 28 and 29 September 2001;
> - Met with four children's organisations – Voice of the Child, Article 12, London Children's Rights Commissioner and Coram Family – to discuss how they might in the first place contribute to the Corporate planning process; and
> - Visited Wales with the Deputy Chair to meet ... National Assembly Minister and ... the Children's Commissioner for Wales ...

The minutes also state under budget:

> The Director of Finance summarised the work on the budget inherited on 1 April 2001 which had been submitted to the Lord Chancellor's Department. The key findings were:
>
> - An identified shortfall of £6.8 million in a full year, which might rise to £9.27 million as a result of ongoing work to identify additional areas of shortfall;
> - The shortfall related to the position on day one and did not take account of additional costs such as harmonisation; and
> - It was unclear whether the CAFCASS budget was a cash budget or a resource budget.
>
> The Chairman said that a separate submission would be made to [the] LCD to deal with resources required to deal with start-up issues.'

The board was informed that headquarters would move to the permanent location of Archway Tower on 14 December 2001.

Later at the same meeting District Judge Nicholas Crichton from the Inner London Family Proceedings Court gave a talk to the board, summarised in the minutes, in which he stressed the importance of the independence of guardians, the value of the tandem model, the contents of the welfare checklist, the responsibilities of guardian and children and

[8] The president of the Family Division and senior family judiciary, plus other guests, met annually. I was invited to speak on behalf of the Department of Health at several such occasions.

family reporters before describing a number of difficult cases he had dealt with.

He felt the enormity of setting up Cafcass had not been appreciated. In the longer term he hoped that Cafcass would be involved in mediation and contact and also contributing to government policy on family matters. He felt strongly that money spent on Cafcass would yield savings in other areas in the longer term but recognised it was a difficult argument to make.

A Board Member's Perspective

Leonie Jordan recollects:

> *It became increasingly evident that a significant consequence of the creation of Cafcass was to prescribe and restrict the independence of self-employed guardians as well as employed guardians and to shift towards a fully or predominantly employed and managed workforce. This inevitably meant a more rigid and bureaucratic organisation, reflecting in the case of care proceedings the deficits to some extent in social work practice in local authorities.*

And also that:

> *While not all guardians worked to a high standard, the majority were professional, resourceful, very experienced and robust on behalf of the child. The tandem model generally worked well, although it was not the cheapest model. The courts – magistrates and judges – were able to rely on the guardian's investigation in partnership with an accredited Children Panel solicitor and their recommendations. Courts were able to push back when there were deficits and gaps in this shared work. Where social workers in LAs were themselves confident and well resourced, effective partnerships produced usually reasonable outcomes for the child. However, the cost was high and one aim it became clear was to restrict the role to reduce increasing costs. But costs rose because of a heavy management structure.*

Reflecting on her board membership, Leonie Jordan comments:

> *The chair was regrettably not agile enough to deal with the at times ruthless politics of Whitehall. The board members, all well intentioned, came from differing backgrounds – rightly – but often could not find common ground. In the end, government intervened and removed the chair and terminated the first board.*

Select Committee on the Adoption and Children Bill

Although the proposed bill would not have radically changed the duties of Cafcass officers in respect of adoption-related applications, there were some significant developments that extended the range of proceedings where they would be appointed to cover the making of an adoption order or a parental responsibility order and signification of consent to placement and adoption. The 2001 bill also gave Cafcass officers new powers to examine and take copies of an adoption agency's records relating to the child and the application and to use these as evidence in court.

Cafcass' chief executive attended the first select committee session on 21 April 2001,[9] less than four weeks after the service had been established. This is another example of early pressure on Cafcass senior management time, as prior briefing and interdepartmental discussion before a select committee attendance would have been necessary. Cafcass' chief executive, as a former chief probation officer, would not have been an expert on adoption-related issues.

In opening the meeting, the committee chairman explained that this was a fairly new procedure and as a committee, they wanted to broadly work through the key elements of the bill and ask specific questions on those matters. He then asked some general introductory questions of the main witnesses. These were several officials from both the Department of Health and the Lord Chancellor's Department, but only the chief executive from Cafcass.

The Department of Health spokesperson explained that adoption laws needed to be looked at again, with some dating from 1976 and others from much earlier. He also explained that following the work done in the early 1990s, there was a general consensus that reform was needed and added: 'We needed in adoption law to put the child right at the very centre of the process in the way that the child has been put in the centre of the Children Act 1989.'

The view from the Lord Chancellor's Department was that the Adoption Bill was a very important step forward in enshrining in legislation the need to manage cases competently and effectively and in a proportionate time frame through the court. It was also stressed that 'the Lord Chancellor's Department will be setting in place arrangements

[9] House of Commons – Select Committee on the Adoption and Children Bill – Minutes of Evidence (parliament.uk)

which will give practical effect to that, and Cafcass will be playing a very important role'. At this point Cafcass' chief executive said she would be particularly keen to ensure that 'something is done to tackle delay and that the voice of the child is heard in the court, and that the interests of the child are paramount'.

Further details about background to the Adoption and Children Act 2002 and its provisions are set out in the explanatory notes[10] accompanying the Act.

Dispute

On 26 June 2001 Community Care's headline was 'CAFCASS Faces Judicial Review'.[11] The article included the following six points, having advised: 'There are some simple observations which those engaged in the conflict might wish to consider.'

> 1. A costing review and job evaluation should be undertaken in an open manner. Clearly the project team which set up CAFCASS did not understand guardian's work. Discussions at regional forums held by CAFCASS have largely produced conflict and anger. The CAFCASS Board need to see the proposed contracts and should be involved in evaluation. What standards are the courts expecting? What will Children Panel solicitors need from guardians in order to provide adequate representation? CAFCASS should at least avoid the appearance of seeking to reduce skill levels.
>
> 2. Children's guardians cannot expect to maintain the same level of independence nor the same unchallenged accounting systems as they have had for the last 20 years.
>
> 3. Local authorities may want to curb the powers of guardians who have exposed too many gaps in practice in the past, but it should be sufficient for future protection against some of the poor guardian practice that has existed, that the new organisation will have an independent management structure to which guardians will be responsible.
>
> 4. The moratorium on implementation of the new contract should be extended indefinitely. The self-employed guardians are a diminishing problem in any event. Clearly CAFCASS will not be employing more people on the existing basis. Too complicated to wait, it is said; the Inland Revenue will not wear it. How about some government?
>
> 5. Get real. In its acknowledgment of service of the permission application, CAFCASS attacked the judicial review application on the basis that the

[10] Adoption and Children Act 2002 – Explanatory Notes (legislation.gov.uk)

[11] CAFCASS faces judicial review – Community Care

decision concerning the contracts was not made by CAFCASS. Whether or not this is legally accurate, it is fatuous. The board through its chairperson and the project team has clearly been engaging in negotiations and offered a contract which they wished to have accepted.

6. The fees per case system is as inappropriate for the work of guardians as the Lord Chancellor eventually accepted it was for solicitors. Two recent developments amply illustrate that the volume and complexity of work make it impossible to ascertain appropriate fee levels in advance.

Judith Timms points out[12] that when Cafcass was established in April 2001 there were 737 self-employed and 117 employed guardians, but by January 2003 there were 522 staff employed on contracts but only 314 self-employed practitioners. She goes on to argue that:

These figures demonstrate a hiatus in the service following CAFCASS' decision to drastically reduce self-employment in July 2001. In addition, the entry qualifications had been reduced from five years' post-qualifying experience to three. Thus, the service was robbed of many of the most experienced guardians who had formed the backbone and helped shape the ethos of the service since 1991.

The Inspectorate's Role

Although the inspectorate kept abreast of the main developments in this painful saga, there was no role that MCSI could officially play in helping to resolve it. I attended a multi-disciplinary conference at Dartington Hall, Devon, in the summer of 2001. The president of the Family Division, Dame Elizabeth Butler-Sloss, and senior Nagalro committee members were also there. I wrote:[13]

The president asked me if I could arrange a quiet room for her and Nagalro to meet later one evening. In the best traditions of 'shuttle diplomacy', I was able to do so. Later I carried a tray of glasses and several bottles of wine across the Dartington lawns to the meeting room. Apart from pouring the wine, I took no part at all in the discussion, but a frank and full exchange of views ensued, which I thought at the time was extremely helpful.

---

[12] https://hansard.parliament.uk/lords/2001-03-27/debates/5d241ff9-0223-42d5-8bfc-12935dfd9319/LordsChamber

[13] Op. cit. 6

Judicial Review

The background and judgment of this important 2001 judicial review are set out below: [14,15]

> From 1 April 2001 onwards, CAFCASS was to determine the terms of the contracts governing all guardians. The Lord Chancellor set up a project team within his department with the aim of settling the guardians' new contractual arrangements for the start of the new service. The team produced a consultation document which proposed that guardians be offered the alternative of an employed or a self-employed contract. However, the Inland Revenue raised serious issues about the definition of self-employment, which led to a reshaping of the contracts. The new draft contracts were, in turn, criticised by the National Association of Guardians ad Litem and Reporting Officers (NAGALRO), which objected to the proposed introduction of graduated fixed fees, arguing that the contract should, instead, be based on an hourly rate. Despite these difficulties, in a series of public statements, CAFCASS and senior government officials confirmed that self-employment would continue to be an option for guardians.
>
> For example, a communication sent by CAFCASS to all guardians on 1 June 2001 stated, inter alia, that it would like to offer guardians the choice between employed and self-employed status. However, on 27 June 2001, following further meetings with NAGALRO, the board of CAFCASS resolved that all guardians should be employed, and that self-employment would not be permitted. The CAFCASS board recorded at the meeting that it wanted a managed service, in the best interests of children and families, and that self-employment in any form was not compatible with a managed service. That decision was posted out, with the offer of a contract of employment, to all guardians on 6 July 2001; a reply was required by 27 July 2001. NAGALRO sought judicial review of the decision, arguing that self-employed guardians had a legitimate expectation that the association, as their representative, would be given an opportunity to make representations prior to any decision being made to exclude the option of self-employment.
>
> **Held** – quashing the decision by CAFCASS to use only employed contracts for guardians – CAFCASS, as a public body, had conducted itself in such a manner as to lead others to believe it was following a particular course, giving rise to a legitimate expectation that a change of course would be preceded by an opportunity for those affected to make representations about why it should not do so. CAFCASS implicitly, by its own conduct, and its

[14] *The Queen on The Application of National Association of Guardians Ad Litem and Reporting Officers v Children and Family Court Advisory and Support Service*, Queen's Bench Division, Scott Baker J, 14 September 2001, Family Law Reports/2002/Volume 1

[15]

> response to the conduct of others, had committed itself to giving reasonable notice that it was thinking of excluding any option of self-employment prior to any decision being made. In failing to give any opportunity for those affected by the CAFCASS decision to exclude self-employment to make representations on the issue, CAFCASS had failed to meet legitimate expectations and had acted unlawfully.

Charles Prest, Director Legal Services at Cafcass, recollects:

> *It was the first day of the first set of judicial review proceedings against Cafcass. I had warned Cafcass' chief executive that it was very likely to be unlawful not to offer any self-employed contract to those who had been guardians ad litem working for the preceding local authority panels, even though those old contracts were now considered by HMRC to look more like contracts of employment than contracts with the self-employed for their services. Yet here we were at the Royal Courts of Justice facing exactly that challenge. I thought wryly about the cash contribution I had made to Nagalro's fighting fund – 'In the interests of justice,' I had said to myself as I made it. Scott Baker J rose. Day 1 was over. Counsel and a group of guardians left the courtroom, and I followed. I still don't know exactly how, but within seconds of stepping through the courtroom door, we knew that something dreadful had happened in New York. It was 11 September 2001.*

Cafcass Funding

The Lord Chancellor's written evidence to the 2003 select committee summarises a developing and complicated picture in the following way:[16]

> The Team developed a budget model for the running costs of the new Service. It covered the on-going costs of frontline practitioners and the new management structure, their accommodation and equipping them including IT provision. This produced a year-one running cost budget of just under £72 million. Year one 'start up' capital money of some nine million pounds was also provided, making a total cash budget of just over £80.8 million.
>
> Much was done to seek to ensure the full cost of predecessor services was transferred into CAFCASS's budget. It was always going to be difficult, however, to take full account of the total costs, including the hidden overheads of support to the many small, locally-delivered services that made up CAFCASS. This was in part because such information was not routinely needed until CAFCASS was in prospect and then not easily obtainable or estimated across numerous localised operations. To ensure it had sufficient funding during its first year, the Department arranged for CAFCASS to use a proportion of its 'start up' money for its running costs.

[16] https://publications.parliament.uk/pa/cm200203/cmselect/cmlcd/614/614w55.htm

> During CAFCASS's second year, 2002–03, the Department increased CAFCASS's running costs funding from the planned £72 million to some £80.5 million. It also allowed CAFCASS to carry forward unspent funding from 2001–02 to give a total operating budget in 2002–03 of some £84.5 million cash.
>
> CAFCASS's budget will also be increased for 2003–04. Our provisional allocation to CAFCASS is £95 million resource; an increase of around £20 million on its year-one running costs budget of £72 million cash. CAFCASS is one of the Department's highest priorities and [the] LCD has shown its commitment to CAFCASS by significantly increasing its funding since launch.

Although the picture painted above is a confident though complex one, there was an alternative view from parts of the field that Cafcass had been underfunded. These contrasting views may be an example of departmental apparent failure to communicate effectively with stakeholders at key moments.

First and Second Years

Written evidence submitted by Cafcass to the committee on the Lord Chancellor's Department is dated 13 March 2003. It may well have been prepared by at least the chairman and the interim chief executive, Jonathon Tross, both of whom also gave oral evidence to the committee on 22 May 2003.[17] The written evidence covers both the first difficult year of Cafcass' operations and a more positive account of its second. In respect of the first year, the evidence stressed that:

> The expectations for CAFCASS were high at the time we were set up and continue to be so now. But creating a cohesive national organisation from 117 previous employing authorities, with different terms and conditions and cultures, was a huge challenge—one that was not fully recognised—but we inherited a highly skilled and experienced workforce, and great commitment to providing an excellent service to children, families and courts…
>
> Many of our staff quite naturally had some anxieties about moving into a new and unknown organisation. But they have enabled us, in the main, to continue to deliver our service. This was acknowledged by the Magistrates' Courts Service Inspectorate (MCSI) in their report 'Setting Up', based on visits in 2001 to all our English regions, Wales, CAFCASS Legal and Headquarters. The Chief Inspector commented '… to the enormous credit of all concerned, front-line services have to a very large extent been maintained.

17 House of Commons – Lord Chancellor's Department – Minutes of Evidence (parliament.uk)

The evidence then highlighted six particular issues that had a significant impact, and these are couched in language which comes across as refreshingly candid:

> The challenge of set-up—CAFCASS was a complex organisation to set up given the number of previous employing authorities, and the timescale from Royal Assent of the relevant legislation to go-live was very short. Overall, the scale of the challenge was underestimated.
>
> Budget—there were concerns that our initial continuing funding level was insufficient. The uncertainty meant we had to be cautious in our first year about entering into future commitments. Since then, the Lord Chancellor's Department have increased significantly our funding.
>
> A lack of infrastructure—we started work with, and still face, gaps in the financial management and human resources systems and other policies that all organisations need...
>
> The self-employed guardians contract—the need to address the issue of the contract was not initiated by us but stemmed from an Inland Revenue indication that the arrangements we inherited were not sustainable. We had, therefore, to review the position. However, the way a new employed contract was planned, and the judicial review proceedings lost because of the lack of proper consultation with those affected, did not aid the culture of mutual respect and confidence we need with our external contractors...
>
> Senior management—we started work without a full senior management team, with number of posts filled on an interim basis. This, and the departure of the Chief Executive and the first Director of Operations, inevitably created difficulties.

Once again, the issue of high expectations is given prominence:

> Our mission was not to stand still but to take the opportunities offered by a merged organisation to improve the service we offered to children and their families. This meant our own staff, as well as our stakeholders in the courts and other public services, were impatient for change. Problems with performance were seen as all the more disappointing against the high expectations.

Leonie Jordan comments about the appointment of the second chief executive on an interim basis:

> *Bringing in a civil servant who had no direct knowledge of the sector to replace ... [the first CEO] ... gave the appearance of some stability but reinforced the increasingly bureaucratic and hierarchical structures with too much focus on procedures and systems rather than nurturing professional*

skills and confidence. One of many examples of this was to implement, against advice, a 'template' for reports to the court over which managers had considerable control/supervision: a failure to understand that an expert witness must be accountable in their own right to the court, not as a representative of a bureaucracy…

Paperwork swamped the board members and meetings, making discussion and guidance on directions and accountability opaque.

Cafcass – One Year On

Richard White also looked back on Cafcass' first operational year,[18] commenting that it had not been a happy one and that its infancy had, on its own admission, been overshadowed by self-inflicted problems. He also points out that 'there is vital developmental work to be done, especially in relation to representation of children in private law cases, supervision of contact and assessment of cases where there has been violence in the family.' White ends with a warning: 'But the government should remember that you cannot give birth to an organisation and then neglect and abuse it without causing serious and significant harm to its long-term welfare.'

Other Experiences

Azora Hurd, as a service manager in Cafcass from 2001 to 2004, recalls that one of the hardest of the transitional arrangements was having to adapt to this new role within the newly established Cafcass.

This entailed having to work within a new regional leadership team made up of some former GALRO panel managers and newly appointed service managers within the West Midlands region … There was very little consideration given to how this new team would work together initially to help manage and lead the service in high demand across the region.

Much of my initial work involved having to sit on several recruitment panels to appoint salaried paid guardians to help meet the shortages within the West Midlands region. As I was the only ethnic-minority service manager at the time, I was expected to sit on nearly all of these interview panels. This did have an impact on me, as it entailed a lot of additional work in notional time allocation and effort that detracted me from the substance of my service manager role … I recall being quite worn out by the process as I tried to balance these expectations whilst trying to meet what the courts and LAs were expecting to be delivered by way of the service.

---

[18] 'Happy Birthday CAFCASS', New Law Journal, 12 April 2002

A Private Law Perspective

Jim Lawson worked in the family justice system from 1986 to 2008 in several roles, including as a senior family court welfare officer in Avon, chief executive of the National Council for Family Proceedings and as a family court adviser in Cafcass. He also co-authored research.[19] He recalls that the creation of Cafcass was an exciting time, although the imperatives around legislation meant that it was 'born before it was conceived', and this resulted in Cafcass having to do more structural and developmental work in the early days of its establishment than was arguably ideal.

Lawson considers that the management structure became increasingly pyramidal, professional training became organisationally prescriptive rather than professionally identified and reports were required to have more internal checks and to be written in an increasingly formulaic way. He saw these changes as the function mainly of an enlarged hierarchy of senior managers, largely drawn from LA social services. He believes they arguably did not understand the ethos of much of the work and consequently felt the need to exert increasing control by introducing procedures and protocols that were felt by many practitioners to be unnecessary and unhelpful and designed as defensive measures.

> There was arguably also an associated belief that child protection was the primary consideration in all areas of the work, a view disputed by many involved in private law work.

But he concludes:

> Despite my misgivings, I think it was right to establish CAFCASS; however, I am left with the feeling it might have provided so much more in welfare terms with creative thinking and sufficient resources.

Cafcass Annual Reports

First Annual Report

On 24 July 2002, in response to a written question to the parliamentary secretary, Lord Chancellor's Department Yvette Cooper's written reply included: 'The Children and Family Court Advisory and Support Service

[19] *Crossing the Boundaries: The Views of Practitioners with Experience of Court Welfare and Guardian Ad litem Work on the Proposal to Create a Unified Welfare Service,* Hunt, J., and Lawson, J., National Council for Family Proceedings, 1999

(Cafcass) has been in existence since April 2001 and will be publishing its first annual report later this year.' [20]

On 23 October 2002, Baroness Hayman asked Her Majesty's Government 'when they intend to publish the Children and Family Court Advisory and Support Service's annual report 2001–02'. The Lord Chancellor, Lord Irvine of Lairg's, written reply said: 'The Children and Family Court Advisory and Support Service (Cafcass) has published its annual report and accounts 2001–02 today. Copies ... have been placed in the libraries of both Houses. Further copies may be obtained from The Stationery Office.'[21]

In response to my request to Cafcass to access its first annual report and accounts (ARA), the Cafcass Governance Team's response dated 23 August 2023 stated: 'We would have physical copies of our ARAs up to 2002; however, they are inaccessible at the moment, as they will be in storage on account of us not having an office space in London.'

Second Annual Report

Baroness Pitkeathley's opening comments to Cafcass' second annual report[22] in 2005 are:

> Looking back over the events of 2004–05, I would describe it as the year when CAFCASS turned a corner and found a fresh sense of purpose, confidence and self-belief. The ultimate beneficiaries of this turnaround are the children and families who use our service.
>
> It began with the arrival of a new Board, and I want to record my grateful thanks to my Deputy Chair, Baroness Howarth and fellow Board members. All have been unswerving in their commitment to build a team with vision, strategic focus and the strength to allow CAFCASS to fulfil its potential at last. No Chair could be more fortunate than I in the calibre of the Board I lead.
>
> Mid-point in the year came another significant event – the arrival of our new Chief Executive. We said goodbye to Jonathan Tross, who had led CAFCASS so ably through a turbulent period, and in September we welcomed Anthony Douglas to his new role. The appointment of someone with such extensive experience of service delivery and personal commitment to children's issues

[20] https://hansard.parliament.uk/commons/2002-07-24/debates/fd5a6e75-ffbe-479f-88e4-5016109e9e74/PerformanceTargets

[21] https://hansard.parliament.uk/Lords/2002-10-23/debates/0774bd54-a987-4095-adef-3eee7b86c6ec/WrittenAnswers

[22] https://www.gov.uk/government/publications/children-and-family-court-advisory-and-support-service-annual-report-and-accounts-2004-to-2005

has been most enthusiastically welcomed by our staff, our sponsoring department, the judiciary and all our partners and colleagues. Anthony has worked tirelessly to get to know the organisation, analyse its difficulties, assess its strengths and inject a fresh sense of energy and vision.

And she continued:

Already I believe we have achieved a much more outward facing and co-operative organisation that is stronger and more able to face the challenges that await us. This is reflected in a more confident relationship with our sponsoring department, the Department for Education and Skills and a positive report from the Constitutional Affairs Select Committee. As the year ends, we welcome a new President of the Family Division – as committed to the potential of CAFCASS as was his predecessor.

The current policy agenda offers us both opportunities and challenges. We have been actively involved in responding to the Green Paper on Parental Separation and the Children and Adoption Bill, and embrace the changing role for our practitioners inherent in these proposals. We share the concerns about resources but know that given proper support our skilled and experienced workforce can and will deliver. We are also working hard to ensure CAFCASS has an active contribution to make to the *Every Child Matters* agenda.

The annual report also comments:

During 2004–05 a renewed sense of purpose and belief has grown within CAFCASS that we can offer a more responsive and effective service to the many children, young people and families we support. Our five key objectives, as agreed by the Secretary of State for Education and Skills, were published in the 2004–05 CAFCASS Business Plan.

OBJECTIVE 1: QUALITY OF SERVICE To safeguard and promote the welfare of children in family proceedings by delivering to CAFCASS service and quality standards
OBJECTIVE 2: BROADER FAMILY SUPPORT To play a proactive part in the government's agenda to support children, young people and their families, looking at ways to develop and improve the support provided.

OBJECTIVE 3: ENGAGING SERVICE USERS To involve and engage children and families to aid our understanding of their diverse needs and to involve them in the development of the service.
OBJECTIVE 4: VALUING AND DEVELOPING STAFF Develop our workforce to ensure all staff are equipped with the necessary skills and support to do their work.

> OBJECTIVE 5: VALUE FOR MONEY Deliver effective governance and management and control of resources to ensure effectiveness and value for money.

Performance in addressing each of the above key objectives is laid out in detail in the report. Addressing workload, the annual report states:

> During the year the various aspects of our work directly impacted on the lives of more than 100,000 children and young people. During this period our teams throughout England and Wales responded to:
> • 13,416 public law cases – these include applications for local authority care and supervision orders and applications for adoption;
> • 38,788 Court-directed Dispute Resolution sessions in private law;
> • 30,813 requests for reports in private law cases – these include applications for parental responsibility, residence and contact, where parents have been unable to reach agreement and 1,141 Rule 9.5 cases under the Family Proceedings Rules (1991), in which a child involved in a private law case is represented by a Guardian ad Litem;
> • 588 Family Assistance Orders, where social work support is provided to families experiencing difficulties after separation or divorce.

And the report goes on to comment:

> Perhaps the most striking trend to emerge during 2004–05 was the sharp increase in the work undertaken by practitioners in Rule 9.5 cases. Here, a child involved in a particularly complex and/or protracted private law case is separately represented under Rule 9.5 of the Family Proceedings Rules (1991). The appointment is as a Guardian ad Litem to the child. These cases more than doubled from last year and take on average up to three times the resource of other private law work, stretching practitioner capacity in some teams. A sample analysis, however, suggests the use of Rule 9.5[23] is proving to be an effective measure in resolving disputes and supporting children in some of our most complex private law cases.

On workforce, the annual report states:

> At the end of 2004–05 we employed 2,060 staff (1,801.35 Whole Time Equivalent), including 1,327 practitioners (1,210.4 WTE). During the year, we contracted the services of 468 self-employed practitioners and employed 51 Bank Scheme staff and two sessional staff, using their skills and experience flexibly across the service.

---

[23] Rule 9.5 is the process by which a child subject to private family proceedings attains party status and the ability to take a proactive stance in the court forum through representation by a guardian ad litem and a solicitor.

Data on Family Proceedings

Cafcass expends a great deal of effort on producing its annual reports, which are statutorily required.[24] Hopefully, all of them will be made available online in due course. Both Cafcass and the government publish a considerable quantity of data at regular intervals on their respective websites.[25] [26] Delay in proceedings and the volume of work undertaken by Cafcass and family courts continue to be among several significant issues. Other questions that may be of continuing relevance include:

- What data might help improve front-line practice?
- What data might point to a need for a change in policy?
- What data might support a case for change in primary or secondary legislation?
- To what other positive purposes might the data be used?
- Does data need to be presented in more suitable formats for different audiences?

Open Board Meetings

An important statutory requirement is that Cafcass 'shall, on at least two occasions in every calendar year, admit members of the public to a meeting of the service, and at one of those meetings the annual report of the service shall be presented.'[27] The format of the meetings has gradually developed since they first started in 2001. Key stakeholder organisations, including the inspectorate, and individual members of the public would typically attend. Some time is allowed for discussion, questions and answers. Board minutes are posted on Cafcass Internet, which also serves as an important resource for children, family and the wider public.

---

[24] Criminal Justice and Court Services Act 2000, Sch 2(12)

[25] https://www.gov.uk/government/statistics/family-court-statistics-quarterly-january-to-march-2023/family-court-statistics-quarterly-january-to-march-2023

[26] https://www.cafcass.gov.uk/about-us/our-data#:~:text=The%20average%20length%20of%20time%20we%20worked%20with%20families%20in%20public%20law%20s31%20applications%20increased%20from%2030%20weeks%20(Q4%202017/18)%20to%2044%20weeks%20(Q4%202020/21)%20and%20currently%20stands%20at%2047%20weeks%20(Q3%202022/23)

[27] The Children and Family Court Advisory and Support Service (Membership, Committee and Procedure) Regulations 2000, https://www.legislation.gov.uk/uksi/2000/3374/regulation/10/made

7

Cafcass and Later Developments

This chapter discusses the House of Commons' Select Committee report of July 2003 and subsequent steps in Parliament and elsewhere to implement significant changes, including seeking Cafcass board resignations and appointing a new board. Giving evidence to a select committee is discussed, as is the handling of concerns raised by one board member by Cafcass, the Civil Service, ministers and a select committee.

Select Committee Report

Compelling detailed evidence is to be found in the 76-page select committee report published in July 2003.[1] Its terms of reference were 'to examine the expenditure, administration and policy of the Lord Chancellor's Department and associated public bodies'.

Seventy-one organisations and individuals submitted written evidence spanning a wide range of interests, professional bodies and other organisations.[2] This documentation runs to 265 pages and well illustrates not only a wide range of opinions but also, in some instances, the anger and frustrations about the alleged shortcomings of Cafcass, the former family court welfare services and the operation of the family courts in dealing with the aftermath of separation and divorce – especially in respect of contact with children. Twenty-eight witnesses were examined in four sessions in April and May 2003, and their evidence can also be accessed on the parliamentary website.

That so many organisations and individuals took the time to submit detailed written evidence illustrates the strength of feelings about a wide range of Cafcass-related issues. For similar reasons, the committee's report and much of the oral evidence deserves to be read in full. The latter often not only illustrates the range of diverse experiences of the former welfare support services, some of which are negative, but also aspirations about what Cafcass should be aiming to achieve. Many submissions also focus

1 House of Commons Committee on the Lord Chancellor's Department Children and Family Court Advisory and Support Service (CAFCASS) Third Report of Session 2002–03 Volume I Report, together with formal minutes

2 House of Commons – Lord Chancellor's Department – Written Evidence (parliament.uk)

on shortcomings in the planning process to establish Cafcass and its performance since vesting day.

Giving Evidence to the Select Committee

Prior to giving oral evidence to the committee in April 2003, the inspectorate had submitted its own written evidence largely based on its inspection visits to Cafcass. There was also the opportunity to attend a government training unit in London.[3]

> The training suite was well equipped, and we watched videos of permanent secretaries and other senior civil servants giving their evidence to select committees ... some did so brilliantly but others dug themselves into great difficulties and floundered ... After some discussion with the trainer, we were put through our paces by him and filmed ... later we watched and discussed the results ... we repeated the process ... It proved to be an invaluable training experience.

Some select committee members may have had relevant professional experience prior to becoming an MP, as did Mr Soley, who was a former Inner London probation officer from 1970 to 1979; a councillor for the London Borough of Hammersmith from 1974 to 1978; a Labour MP from 1979 to 2001; and from 2005 a Life Peer. As MPs, all may have had experiences of Cafcass brought to their local constituency surgeries. The report's introduction mentions that a number of the select committee members undertook visits to Cafcass offices in their local areas.

Although witnesses might do their best to anticipate what questions might be asked, they also need to ensure that their strongest points are made as effectively as possible. My oral evidence to the select committee[4] on 8 April 2003 as one of its first witnesses from the MCSI included the following exchanges with Mr Clive Soley. Its inclusion in full may help illustrate some of the challenges one faces in dealing with complex issues succinctly in response to a series of unseen questions.

Better or Worse?

> 14. You have described an organisation that is getting better. If I asked you to provide a photograph of where it is at now and compare it to the situation before CAFCASS was created, would you say that a child going through the system now had a better chance of getting the right decision in the right timescale or a worse chance?

[3] Op. cit. 6

[4] House of Commons – Lord Chancellor's Department – Minutes of Evidence (parliament.uk)

(Mr Poyser) When we talk about the situation before CAFCASS started ... I think we need to be clear that there was pretty poor data around the country as to exactly what was happening. Nevertheless ... in parts of the country children now in the first two years of CAFCASS have experienced an unacceptably worse service, but there have been a lot of regional variations and variations within regions which need to be picked up. There are some risks about generalising across the whole of England and Wales. One of the problems about having difficulties at a local level is that if there is a shortfall in Cornwall, for example, it is not much help having extra staff in Bristol, which is still within the same region, because they cannot physically get down to Cornwall and replacing staff and the rest of that degree of flexibility in practical terms poses certain problems.

15. So if I asked you to provide a table of regions as to how well it is doing, obviously to some extent it would be impressionistic, could you give such a table?

(Mr Poyser) I do not think we could on the basis of our inspections because our inspections took place at different times throughout 2002–03 and therefore it would be a very distorted table. If one takes the narrow issue of unallocated cases, when we were in the East Midlands recently ... at that moment they were not facing unallocated cases, although they were warning that they might do before too long. In January we were in the South East ... and there are significant pockets of unallocated work there, but that would only be one factor that ought to be in any theoretical league table perhaps.

16. Do you think you ought to try and get to a situation where you could give us some idea of that on a regional basis?

(Mr Poyser) ... The whole question of league tables within the CAFCASS regions or between teams in CAFCASS is an important and interesting concept and one which clearly has been pursued more broadly in the public services. We have given it some initial thought and we think at the moment one of the issues that would make it really difficult ... is the absence of robust management information to describe precisely what is going on and what are the factors that ought to contribute. I would not rule it out in the medium term either for the Inspectorate or for CAFCASS itself to collect data in a way which allowed fair comparisons between units of its operation, whether they be teams or regions, but there are certain risks.

17. Taking you back to my first question, you are implying that in some areas the child might get a better service than before and in some areas worse. Is that right?

(Mr Poyser) I did not mean to imply that any would be getting a better service. What we said in our first Report, Setting Up, was that in terms of volume

and quality, remembering that the new service was meant to be applying the inherited standards, then many children would have got the same sort of service as before and not better. I recall vividly going to see one care centre judge in the early days, and he said, 'What change? I had a very good service before CAFCASS. I've got a very good service now.' In that area ... there was high judicial satisfaction at that time six months into CAFCASS.

18. But if you are acknowledging that the photograph now would not be as good as it should be in effect, is this due to the quality of the decision or the time taken? There are two things that affect a child in this respect. It is whether the right decision is taken with the right judgment being made, and the other one is the period of time that it might take in which the child might be expected to put up with inadequate secondary provision for a period of time.

(Mr Poyser) I think there are a number of interacting factors, and they will weigh differently in different situations. There is the delay in allocating cases that clearly need to be allocated straightaway. There is the quality of staff and whether with experience they can get on with the job effectively and perform their role vis-a-vis the children, the families and the courts. There are also wider environmental issues in relation to what is happening generally to proceedings in that area as far as delay and duration are concerned, the availability of experts, the time-tabling of the courts and the wider situation. As far as CAFCASS is concerned, the three most important would be the availability of staff, the quality of staff and the internal quality supervision of staff.

19. Can I ask you a final question on the quality of the reports that are prepared compared to the decision prior to CAFCASS. In reading those reports, which I presume you do on a sampling basis, would you say the samples that you read now are of a higher quality than the ones that were done before CAFCASS, the same or worse?

(Mr Poyser) We ourselves never read reports before CAFCASS, and so the evidence about what they were like historically is somewhat anecdotal. During our inspections we read routinely in each region about 120 reports, both public and private [law], so we have built up a knowledge of several hundred reports so far. What we find is that at one end of the spectrum there is superb work and at another level there is certainly good enough work, but occasionally we come across recent reports where we are left with some doubt about the quality ... and we would have thought in some of those reports the courts would have been less than satisfied.

20. Surely there is a case for you looking back historically to see whether or not services have got better or worse.

(Mr Poyser) There is a case for looking at historical reports. There would be issues about what standards those reports should be judged against just as there is now. What might have been good enough … five years or seven years ago might not be acceptable now, as one hopefully becomes more demanding about standards.

21. They might be better.

(Mr Poyser) They could have been better or they might have been insensitive to diversity issues, to human rights issues or on the focus of the child, all of which have certainly been of a higher profile in more recent times.

Others Experiences

Liz Goldthorpe recalls writing in the Association of Lawyers for Children (ALC) Newsletter in July 2003. This covered her experience not only of giving evidence to the select committee in May 2003 as ALC's chair but also having earlier submitted written evidence on the Association's behalf, focusing on public law and also having taken soundings from across the ALC committee and various practitioners around the country.

At that time, she was working as a specialist child care lawyer in Manchester and also as a tribunal judge. Her article notes:

> Although a Select Committee can only make recommendations, this was clearly an unmissable opportunity to air in detail the service crisis in the representation of children and young people and the continuing breaches of their human rights.
>
> I went armed with Richard White whose series of articles on CAFCASS had been found 'most useful' by the Committee … Evidence in court is one thing; going past heavy police security, and the spot where King Charles was tried, to address a House of Commons Select Committee is quite another experience altogether. However, we were treated very courteously by an extraordinarily well-informed committee … 35 minutes … passed speedily indeed.

Liz Goldthorpe also comments in the article:

> The Committee is, of course, briefed by a very experienced committee clerk and their special advisers Professor Judith Masson of Warwick University and Professor Adrian James of Bradford University, but they seemed to know a great deal about the inner workings of the debacle.

The ALC article makes some interesting and indeed prescient observations about an earlier event in 2003, explaining, 'This had been preceded by a reception on 1 April to launch the LCD select committee and to meet members of the committee (extremely helpful if you are about to be grilled by them) ... but also to have some input into suggestions about what topics the committee might tackle next. Given the size of the LCD, the possibilities are endless of course, but immigration and public funding may prove irresistible.'

Liz Goldthorpe recalls that the ALC was regularly consulted on a wide range of child law issues and had a wealth of evidence, so she felt confident its contribution would be treated as important. She thought the resulting select committee report was thorough and inspired and hoped that Cafcass 'would emerge as a really positive, well-planned, child-focused organisation that preserved the expertise and independence of the GAL service', although she concludes, 'Sadly, that proved misplaced.'

Commenting on family support services before Cafcass, Liz Goldthorpe suggests that much of this early period was encouraging. 'High-quality child-focused services based on good practice seemed not only possible but actually existed in places ... and was being promoted by the senior judiciary. A multidisciplinary approach with good-quality training, and independent scrutiny of executive decision-making was the gold standard that seemed to be accepted as the goal. However, it became obvious in later years that such efforts were increasingly falling away under the pressure of cuts and the promotion into senior positions of professionals with either no experience of child law issues or no interest in pursuing them (or both).'

And Judith Timms' recollections include:

> *CAFCASS was established with high hopes for the new organisation. However, it soon became clear that the first board members and CEO were not fit for purpose and there were deep concerns across the sector about the deterioration in the service to children. In March 2003 I and many other witnesses gave damning evidence of CAFCASS' poor performance to the select committee.*

As noted later, Judith Timms was appointed to the Cafcass board in 2004.

Select Committee Report

The 2003 select committee report's opening summary sets out some powerful messages:

> The skill and devotion of staff throughout the organisation and their commitment to the children they serve is not to be gainsaid, and criticisms of the way CAFCASS's difficulties have been handled should not detract from

that. Nevertheless, widespread concern about CAFCASS's performance has been apparent ever since it was set up. A dispute with the self-employed guardians who made up the bulk of the pre-CAFCASS workforce on the public law side of the new organisation's work led to a loss of staff, which had a serious impact on CAFCASS's ability to deliver core services. CAFCASS found itself unable to cope with increasing demand for its services and significant delays in the allocation of guardians to cases persisted. Meanwhile, CAFCASS failed to improve the service offered by the Family Court Welfare Service in private law disputes. Many vulnerable children were left without full representation at critical times as a result.

It continues:

Our inquiry found serious failings in the establishment and management of the new Service. Too little time was allowed for its establishment, leaving the organisation at a disadvantage from the start. Once established, CAFCASS failed to make proper use of the preparatory work which had been done, compounding the difficulties. Relations with self-employed guardians were mishandled, resulting in the alienation of an important sector of the workforce. The focus on the dispute and an over-emphasis on the creation of management structures led to the neglect of other important aspects of the service, including training and professional development, IT and the development of support services for children and families experiencing relationship breakdown. Meanwhile, the delivery of CAFCASS's core services failed to improve.

And the report judges that:

A CAFCASS Board lacking experience and expertise in key areas of the organisation's work proved unable to exercise effective oversight or provide appropriate strategic direction, hindered by confusion over lines of accountability and the respective roles of the Board, the senior management team and the Lord Chancellor's Department. The dismissal of the original Chief Executive caused further disruption to CAFCASS's work, while [the] LCD itself managed to create the impression that its prime interest in the new Service was in keeping costs down.

Other funding issues are addressed in the report, which says:

The inherent problems of setting up a new organisation and difficulties in the provision of core services are not, however, the only reason why progress in the development of support services has been slow. CAFCASS has suffered significant budget constraints in its early period. Indications are that recent increases have now brought CAFCASS close to a level where it has sufficient funds to meet its core responsibilities (although even this is not certain, hence

> our recommendation above regarding the conduct of a detailed workforce planning exercise).

The report also comments:

> If CAFCASS is to make a significant long-term contribution to the development of support services, however, we expect the Department will need to increase funding further. Any such investment would not be wasted ... a properly functioning expanded CAFCASS will result in substantial savings in other areas of the system—fewer contested court proceedings, with consequential substantial savings in both time and money spent in court, without counting the more intangible emotional benefits to children and families brought about by the amicable resolution of contact disputes.

The committee makes a number of recommendations aimed at 'enabling Cafcass to become the high-quality service operating to the best professional standards envisaged when it was first proposed'. The committee continues:

> The priority for CAFCASS must be for it to get to grips with its service delivery duties and clear the backlog of cases which has been allowed to build up. To assist in doing so, it should conduct a comprehensive workforce planning exercise aimed at ensuring that it knows what resources are needed. It should establish a dedicated training and professional development strand and enable the effective performance management of its front-line practitioners. It should put in place a fully-fledged case management system which will allow the collation of reliable information for management and research purposes and relieve some of the burden on hard-pressed front-line managers. It should indicate the role it envisages for itself in the provision of support services and develop relations with other bodies working in the field, particularly the Legal Services Commission. Additionally, it should develop its research capacity so that it can establish 'what works' for children experiencing family breakdown.

The committee also stresses:

> Changes are also required in corporate governance. CAFCASS needs to demonstrate clearly and unambiguously that it is putting children and young people first in all it does. It should re-examine its management structures with a view to ensuring that it has a management style appropriate to the work it does. CAFCASS's Framework Document should be rewritten so that it explicitly reflects the Service's core tasks and sets out the proper constitutional relationship between CAFCASS as an NDPB and its parent Department. There should be a fundamental review of membership of the Board, with the aim of bringing onto it people of experience and stature who can develop

> the strategy necessary to deliver an effective, child-centred service. The new Board should take steps to ensure that it is able to carry out effectively its function of providing strategic direction and holding senior management to account.

The committee concludes:

> CAFCASS performs a vitally important function in the protection of vulnerable children at a critical time in their lives. In the two years of its existence so far, considerable doubt has been cast on its ability to perform that function effectively. CAFCASS needs to be helped to use, develop and build on the considerable skills which exist among its personnel and to become the kind of quality organisation it was originally intended to be. We hope that by addressing the concerns raised in this Report CAFCASS will begin to regain the confidence of those working with and for it and show that it is an organisation genuinely and effectively committed to the children it serves.

The report's penultimate chapter is titled 'The Way Forward'. It states in stark language:

> The situation we have described ... is not a happy one. It shows an organisation which is respected neither by all its own staff nor by many of its partners and stakeholders; which is failing to provide its core services in a timely and effective manner; and which has been unable to make any progress in fulfilling the hopes expressed for it in providing new and coordinated support services for children and families experiencing relationship breakdown...
>
> This picture does not fully do justice to the good work which has been done both by individual practitioners and, to some extent, by senior management since the Service was established. Even following the bleakest period in CAFCASS's history, in the months after set-up, MCSI was able to report that 'front-line services [had] to a very large extent been maintained' ... 'the storm has abated and patches of blue sky are beginning to appear ... A strategy is now emerging which will lead ... to a more effective, better managed service in future years...
>
> Those of us who have visited individual CAFCASS regions have seen that view reflected in the attitude of staff and management who are now gaining confidence in the ability of the organisation to set itself properly on its feet ... In many ways the views which have been expressed by our witnesses reflect the CAFCASS of a year ago, rather than the CAFCASS of today.

The select committee's final chapter, 'Conclusions and Recommendations', repeats some of the material highlighted in its earlier chapters, which also make recommendations. Confusingly for readers, the report does not list all its 47 recommendations in one place, some being in the final chapter and others appearing in earlier ones.

Departmental Changes

Following the machinery of government changes announced by the prime minister in June 2003, responsibility for Cafcass would transfer to the Department for Education and Skills (DfES), under the Minister for Children.[5]

For different reasons, this may have come as some relief to both the LCD and Cafcass. The Lord Chancellor's Department became the Department for Constitutional Affairs (DCA),[6] although for unknown reasons there was a delay between the June 2003 announcement and the enabling transfer order made in January 2004. Ten years later another change took place when in 2014 responsibility for Cafcass in England transferred from the Department for Education (DfE) to the Ministry of Justice (MoJ).

Parliamentary Response

The first parliamentary response to the July 2003 select committee report was the Westminster Hall debate held on 23 October 2003.[7] It was scheduled for two and a half hours and was opened by the select committee chairman,[8] who said:

> I am glad to have the opportunity to open this debate, and to welcome the Minister to her new post.[9] She can bear no responsibility for what has gone before, but we place on her a heavy responsibility to use her new position to see that things run a great deal better in future. We have high hopes.

A wide number of contributions were made by MPs and the minister before the committee chairman in his summing up at the close of the debate said it was important 'for us and for others to revisit relatively soon the issues that we have discussed today to ensure that nothing is lost sight of.' He added:

---

[5] On 12 January 2004 a Transfer of Functions Order transferred formal responsibility for CAFCASS to DfES.

[6] On 1 April 2014 responsibility for Cafcass in England transferred from the Department for Education to the Ministry of Justice.

[7] https://api.parliament.uk/historic-hansard/westminster-hall/2003/oct/23/children-and-family-court-advisory-and

[8] Rt Hon Alan Beith MP, Liberal Democrat, Berwick-upon-Tweed

[9] Margaret Hodge MP, Labour, Barking

> It is fair to say that board members have tried to challenge what was going on in the organisation, and that the board as a whole was handicapped from the start ... individual board members will obviously carry the burden of what they know ... they have become increasingly aware of some of the things going wrong with CAFCASS.

He then commented:

> The Minister diligently responded to a wide range of the issues raised [about resources] ... She was asking how we had got into the present situation, given that everything was done at a much lower cost before.

And that:

> If I remember rightly, it was discovered at quite an early stage – once it was established just who was working for CAFCASS and how many people were involved – that the salaries bill almost exceeded the base budget set for the organisation. Quite how that happened is a mystery to me, but it illustrated that there was something seriously wrong in resourcing from the beginning.

He further commented:

> The Minister will have to knock pretty hard on the Treasury's door, if only to tell it that something must be done to alleviate the situation immediately, which will require some resources. Hopefully, there need not be a permanent shift in the balance, but there are immediate resourcing needs.

And then added:

> Government reorganisation ... need not prevent the start of work to get the framework document rewritten and to establish a new culture in how the Department relates to the organisation. We need to create, through the appointment of a new board, an organisation that takes responsibility for its decisions and is allowed to get on with the job with the necessary resources, without having constantly to respond to ambiguous instruction from the parent Department.

The chairman's final comments were:

> There must be effective use of the skills that are available to CAFCASS, or that could become available if it recruits, or brings back in, the people who are outside. Above all, the service must put the children first.

The Government Response

The government response to the select committee report[10] in October 2003 is a detailed 31-page document presented in two parts – first from ministers to the recommendations directed at the government by the select committee and second from the Cafcass board addressing the recommendations the committee made to it.

As with the select committee report, the response justifies reading in full in order to appreciate the range of issues addressed. Early on the report importantly records:

> Its appreciation and agreement with the Committee's comments in its report about the dedication and commitment of CAFCASS professionals who have continued to provide services to the vulnerable children CAFCASS serves. It is a tribute to these professionals and the all CAFCASS staff that these vital services to children have continued to be provided.

As a broad generalisation, each response given in the government document is positive in tone and where necessary offers either an explanation for the decision made or signals future intent and commitment in a specific direction.

Delay in Public Law Cases

In 2003 the concerns about delay led the Lord Chancellor to set up an advisory committee on judicial case management in public law Children Act cases. As its membership listed in Appendix Two reflects, this was almost entirely about high-level processes and seems to make the basic assumption that if the judiciary took greater control in the management of cases, other agencies would necessarily have to fall into line. Initially, there was a consensus to move to a protocol, but in practice it did not produce all the desired results and delay continued to remain a matter of the greatest concern for many following years.

Resignation

The resignation of the Cafcass board's first chair became effective on 13 October 2003, and another board member was appointed as interim chair. Following up one of the select committee's recommendations, Sir Clive

[10] The Response of the Government and the Children and Family Court Advisory and Support Service to the Constitutional Affairs Select Committee's Report on the Children and Family Court Advisory and Support Service (CAFCASS), presented to Parliament by the Secretary of State for Constitutional Affairs October 2003, Cm 6004

Booth, a former chairman of the Teacher Training Agency, was asked by ministers to review the Cafcass board in the light of criticism that it had too little experience of the child welfare and family court system.

Media Views

The Guardian[11] reported on this development with the headline 'Cafcass Inquiry Head Lacks Experience, Say Critics' and said of the Booth Review:

> His review, which is understood to be underway, is expected to take less than a month. He has been asked to carry out a 'fundamental review of the membership board' of Cafcass [by] the interim director of Margaret Hodge's new Children and Families Directorate.

The news story continues:

> Part of Sir Clive's review will be to 'consider the qualities, type and level of skill, desirable background and depth of experience needed for the board ... It should consider whether the existing membership of the Cafcass board match those requirements.

And further states:

> Alison Paddle ... chairwoman of ... Nagalro, said that while she could not comment on Sir Clive's appointment specifically, she was concerned the person appointed should have an understanding of what the job of a children's guardian entails. 'We would want the people involved in this to be very much in touch with what is quite a complex field and to be able to come up with something that really is going to make strong and substantial changes.

However, the article concludes:

> A spokesperson for the DfES is quoted: '[Sir Clive] has been appointed to look at how the board operates ... it has nothing to do with families and children ... He is not looking at Cafcass specifically but how the board operates and how it needs to work.

This comment may have struck some readers as rather controversial.

More Resignations

Sir Clive Booth reported on 9 November 2003 and advised that the board needed a fresh start and all members should be invited to tender their resignations. The Lord Chancellor wrote to all Cafcass board members on

---

[1] https://www.theguardian.com/society/2003/oct/22/childrensservices

2 December 2003 asking them to resign. This was reported on 8 December by Community Care, which said:[12]

> The board of the crisis-hit Children and Family Court Advisory and Support Service has been told to resign by the government. An independent review of the board membership by Sir Clive Booth led to the demand from Lord Chancellor Lord Falconer, and steps have already been taken to appoint a new board and chairperson. A government spokesperson said: 'All Cafcass board members have been asked to resign. We would like to pay tribute to the hard work and dedication of the board to Cafcass during its first years.'

In response to the Lord Chancellor's letter of 2 December to all board members asking them to resign, the DfES permanent secretary spoke to all five board members on 9 December who at that point had not resigned. By the following day all but two board members had resigned, and by 11 December one further board member had resigned, leaving only one member who had not done so.

On 11 December 2003 the Secretary of State for Constitutional Affairs and Lord Chancellor made a statement, which included:

> The Minister for Children, Young People and Families ... has today announced ... that Baroness Pitkeathley OBE has been appointed as chairman of CAFCASS, with effect from 11 December 2003 ... all but one member of the existing board have agreed to resign ... As an interim measure Baroness Pitkeathley will be assisted by a temporary board ... We will be placing advertisements shortly for appointment to a new permanent board ... The board member who has declined to resign is being asked to accept the suspension of their board membership, pending further consideration of their position.

Cafcass' Temporary Board

In the light of all the autumn 2003 events summarised above, it was inevitable that the fresh start referred to was indeed urgently required at many levels. In 2003 Professor Jane Tunstill headed the social work department at Royal Holloway College, London University, when she was approached about the temporary board. She recalls in about December:

> *I came back to my office one day to find a message to call a senior civil servant who said the minister wanted to discuss something with me ... the first thing to enter my head was panic ... some negative issue about my role in social work education ... universities walked on political eggshells in those*

[12] Cafcass board told to resign – Community Care

> *days ... All was revealed ... would I be prepared to join the transitional board ... established to replace the existing one ... obviously I said yes.*

Professor Tunstill also recalls the temporary board's priorities and how it worked.

> *Our initial task under discussion was the importance ... of ensuring the appointment of a permanent appropriately qualified chief executive ... My overwhelming recollection was of the skill, efficiency, charm and strategic brilliance which Jill Pitkeathley brought to the role ... We were a collaborative, mutually respectful little group.*

New Appointments

Meanwhile, changes at the top of Cafcass' management were swift. A new chief executive – Anthony Douglas – was also appointed to replace Jonathon Tross, whose tenure was understood to have been as an interim, although invaluable, measure.

A new chair and new board members, including those from the temporary board, were appointed early in 2004 and were due to take up their role in April. Again, questions might be posed about the new appointments over and above those previously appointed to the temporary board – for example, who drew up the shortlisted applicants; who sat on the interview panels; how many applicants and from what backgrounds applied and how many were turned down; and how was diversity addressed?

Details of the new board membership are set out in Appendix One.

Regulatory Changes

There were a number of changes introduced by the Department for Education and Skills (DfES) in 2005.[13] Its explanatory memorandum comments that following the transfer of Cafcass' functions in Wales to the National Assembly, there was no longer a need for a board member to represent Welsh interests. Other changes include new powers for the Secretary of State to suspend members, as well as to remove them from office, and similar powers are given to Cafcass in respect of its co-opted appointees.

Perhaps reflecting the difficulties discussed later in chapter 11 with a dissenting board member, it was recognised that the power to suspend

[13] Children and Family Court Advisory and Support Service (Membership, Committee and Procedure) Regulations 2005 no.433

was omitted from the old 2001 regulations as an oversight, and the new provision rectified this. The new power to suspend also enables the Secretary of State (and Cafcass) to undertake investigations and allow the board member to make representations before a final decision on removal is made. The grounds for the Secretary of State to remove a board member from office are specified in the old regulations in rather limited terms – namely, non-attendance at meetings and where the member was unfit or unable to perform his duties. However, in practice these proved to be restrictive, and a new ground, covering circumstances in which it is not in the interests of Cafcass for a member to continue to hold office, has been provided.

To bring Cafcass in line with current practice in other non-departmental public bodies, other new regulations required members who have an interest in a matter brought up for consideration at meetings of Cafcass to disclose that interest and not to participate in meetings at which that matter is discussed.

Further regulations give a representative of the Secretary of State and the chief executive officer (CEO) of Cafcass a right to attend all meetings of Cafcass and its audit committee. The previous constitution had allowed Cafcass to co-opt the CEO and the Secretary of State's representative, but this meant they became members of Cafcass, which DfES considered inappropriate. The new provision also prohibits them from taking part in the decision-making process. There was also a provision that allowed employees to be co-opted members of the board, and this has been removed, as it is inappropriate for employees to be members of the service, since there could be possible conflicts of interest. The provision requiring Cafcass to have a finance committee has been removed, since there was some duplication of work between the committee and the audit committee.

Cafcass' First Chair

In an exchange of letters with me in 2015, Anthony Hewson's reflections on Cafcass' first year[14] as its first chairman included:

> I am sorry you were reminded once again of … 'the very painful early period of Cafcass'. It's one of two parts of my life I would rather forget. But we are where we are. I have and continue to admire greatly the work of Anthony

[14] Anthony Hewson died on 30 June 2021. The Guardian carried an obituary, https://www.theguardian.com/society/2021/aug/04/anthony-hewson-obituary

Douglas[15] although I have never met him ... It's also true to say that some Cafcass people keep their distance because it was of course a very bruising experience for us all. That is a view I respect and some are of course still dealing with the consequences.

Another Perspective

June Thoburn was a professor at the University of East Anglia from 1989 to 2004. She was a Cafcass board member from 2009 to 2012 and also a special adviser to Cafcass from 2011 to 2017. Her recollections help to illustrate how an effective board should operate.
She recalls:

> *I joined Cafcass board after the previous chair board and chief executive had resolved the previous start-up issues ... there was a richness of experience from strong minded people with both executive and non-executive members willing to put in the work and in preparing for full boards and sub-committees.*

And she continues:

> *Board meetings were well prepared by staff and well managed by chairs. These were meetings I looked forward to ... there was space for discussion as well as decision-making and everyone, as far as I can tell, spoke their mind.*
>
> *The chief executive and his strong team had the required range of professional skills to manage the day-to-day work, sometimes very complex as with the problematic introduction of a new IT service ... There was a good balance with experienced local politicians, legally qualified, experience senior managers and social workers with research and practice experience ... Non-executive board members and chief executive were not always of one mind but very comfortable in airing disagreements ... Members of the young people's board started to attend meeting ... a welcome development ...*
>
> *Board meetings were not without their challenging moments. I recall at least one occasion when the Cafcass team came to the board with a well-worked out plan and when non-executives put up strong arguments about why this might not be a good idea ...*
>
> *Particular positive memories are of the wisdom of those members who brought in their expertise from local government/politics/business/ finance/law and were attentive listeners and challengers.*

---

[5] Anthony Douglas was Cafcass' Chief Executive Officer from 2004 to 2019.

Professor Thoburn's other positive memories are of the away days, which allowed for broader issues of policy and practice to be debated, and the dinners at which informal views could be shared among ourselves, senior staff and key 'stakeholders' (e.g. the president of the Family Division). These were coming to an end as she left – with finances increasingly limited – a false economy in her view.

8

The UN Convention on the Rights of the Child

This chapter addresses aspects of the UN Convention on the Rights of the Child (UNCRC), the role of the Department of Health and some links with the voice of the child in family court proceedings, as well as the Human Rights Act 1988 and the Children's Commissioner.

The Convention on the Rights of the Child

During the 1990s, the Department of Heath held the UK-wide lead for reporting on the United Nations Convention on the Rights of the Child. I was given responsibility for the production of the UK's Second Report[1] and, leading a small team of civil servants, worked closely with the voluntary sector as well as officials in Scotland, Wales and Northern Ireland.

Article 12 has particular relevance for the welfare support services. It states:

> 1. States Parties shall assure to the child who is capable of forming his or her own views the right to express those views freely in all matters affecting the child, the views of the child being given due weight in accordance with the age and maturity of the child.
> 2. For this purpose, the child shall in particular be provided the opportunity to be heard in any judicial and administrative proceedings affecting the child, either directly, or through a representative or an appropriate body, in a manner consistent with the procedural rules of national law.

A UNCRC Conference

An article titled 'Presenting a United Front'[2] began:

> It's not every day you get representatives from government departments across the UK rubbing shoulders with people from children's organisations as diverse as the NSPCC, Childline, Barnardo's, National Children's Bureau and the Children's Rights Office and with children themselves.

Convention on the Rights of the Child – Second Report to the UN Committee on the Rights of the Child by the United Kingdom, 1999

Children's Services News, April/May 1998

And continued:

> But it's not every day that a conference on the UN Convention on the Rights of the Child is staged. The purpose of the conference held in February at Skipton House was essentially to kick off the consultative process which will lead to the Government publication of a comprehensive report on children's rights in England, Northern Ireland, Scotland and Wales.
>
> All countries who have ratified the United Nations Convention are obliged to produce such a document for the Committee in Geneva, and this is the second time – 1994 being the first – that a report has to be prepared.
>
> The conference's main aim therefore, says Arran Poyser, conference organiser, was to provide a forum for 'brainstorming and an opportunity to re-affirm that all these groups can work together despite sometimes having different opinions'.
>
> To this end, 85 delegates including 15 children turned up to Skipton House with a brief:
>
> - to discuss what had been achieved so far and what needs to be improved upon or introduced
> - to develop partnerships between government and non-government organisations
> - to decide what areas might be viewed as contentious
> - to timetable the various stages leading to the report
>
> An advisory group was also established to help write the report. Following an opening speech by Health Minister Paul Boateng, who re-emphasised that children need to be at the heart of the report, delegates were divided into groups. Each had the specific task of deciding how best to involve children throughout the year and which elements concerning children were considered beneficial. These details were fed back into a plenary session later on in the morning. Several presentations, including one delivered by the children themselves, were held throughout the day. A key theme is to ensure that the report is accessible to children and of use to practitioners around the country.

Preparing for this conference encountered difficulties from an unexpected quarter. A few days before it was due to take place, I was telephoned by a Number 10 special adviser. In 2001 I wrote that he said:

> 'We could not possibly have such an event and we were not to talk to anyone. The government had not yet decided about its children's rights policy and UNCRC'. I explained firmly that this was a retrospective account mainly covering the work under the Conservative government and was not about future promises from Labour. Tempers frayed especially when I suggested he

didn't know what he was talking about and he rang off. I alerted a very senior civil servant at the department, and the same special adviser was soon in contact with him. I do not know what was discussed but I was instructed to contact by FAX all the civil servant attendees from across the UK to inform them that they had to arrive early for a special pre-conference meeting. We crowded into a room and were warned by the department's senior civil servant that on all accounts we had to be careful what we said in front of non-civil-servants that day ...

My departmental colleague Deidre Correa recalls her own important contribution:

A small but dedicated team helped to commission and coordinate the contributions from the many government departments across England, Wales, Scotland and Northern Ireland. Not forgetting the invaluable partnership of the non-government organisations too. As the deadline for its publication was approaching many an hour was spent proofing and re-proofing final drafts. It was a truly Herculean task, and something to be very proud to have been a part of.

Although for legal and technical reasons the legislation does not mention the UNCRC, its underlying spirit accords with some of the convention's principles. When Paul Boateng MP[3] was a junior minister at the Department of Health in 1998, I wrote:[4]

Arranging for him to meet the Norwegian Children's Ombudsman who was visiting London. He described his role and the many advantages of the Norwegian system. Mr Boateng was very attentive and asked a number of questions. The meeting ended with the Children's Ombudsman presenting Mr Boateng with his book about his work which Mr Boateng promised to read. I then said to the minister 'I didn't know you could read Norwegian.' ... Luckily, everyone laughed.

Christine Smart worked as a children's guardian from 1997 to 2003 before being promoted within Cafcass to senior management roles and becoming Cafcass' first children's rights director. She recalls:

The positive shift in front-line practice in its core function to hearing the views and feelings of children and presenting these to the court ... this was especially important with children whose parents were divorcing and were caught up in the distress of this broken, fraught adult relationship.

---

[3] Elected MP for Brent South in 1987. Created Baron Boateng in 2010.

[4] Op. cit. 6

However, in Cafcass' first year, UNCRC concerns were not prominently addressed at a policy level, although they continued to be reflected in much front-line practice, perhaps often undertaken implicitly rather than expressed explicitly.

In my 2001 paper I recall[5] speaking about the UK's preparation of its report for the UNCRC at a UNICEF-organised[6] conference in 1999 in Barbados attended by all the Caribbean countries:

> I repeated to the UK High Commissioner who came to some of the conference my concern that in my work I had not come across a single official working full time on UNCRC matters within the Civil Service in Britian, yet Jamaica had three.

When discussing the UNCRC in 2001, I noted then that[7] the 'UNCRC had a rather low profile in the UK. It is not generally used as a working document to help frame our policies or day-to-day practices. Copies of the convention are not usually in evidence on the desks of officials, ready to be consulted daily.'

Responsibility

When the 221-page report was published with executive summaries in both English and Welsh, the position of the non-government organisations (NGOs) and the government was clarified:

> 1.9.1 The Government of the United Kingdom records its gratitude to the many NGOs who have contributed to the preparation of this report. They have had a considerable influence on its content, and the Government hope that many of them will see their points reflected in it. But the report as submitted to the United Nations must, under the terms of the Convention, be a report by the Government of the United Kingdom. The Government does not expect NGOs to share responsibility for the report, or to be bound by its content. Responsibility for this report rests exclusively with the Government.

The Second Report has no discussion of Article 12 and its relevance in family court proceedings in England and Wales. This is because in 1999 there was little new to report on the framework of the Galro service provision across England and Wales compared with what had been covered five years earlier in the UK's First Report produced in 1994 after the implementation of the Children Act 1989 in 1991.

---

[5] Op. cit. 6

[6] UNICEF – United Nations International Children's Emergency Fund

[7] Op. cit. 6

A UNCRC Celebration

To mark the tenth anniversary of the UNCRC, I arranged a celebratory conference in November 1999, which departmental colleagues from the Department of Health and the Lord Chancellor's Department helped organise. The venue was Lancaster House in London, which had also been used to mark the implementation of the Children Act 1989 in October 1991. Among the 300 invited guests were senior civil servants, Galro panel managers and half a dozen ministers, who all spoke briefly, as did an excellent children's group who were supported by a national voluntary child care organisation.

A Later Perspective

In contrast to some of my 1999 views on the low profile of the UNCRC quoted above, Adrian James, writing some years later in 2007,[8] argues that although the UNCRC has yet to be incorporated into domestic legislation and therefore does not have the full force of UK law, it has had a more far-reaching impact since its ratification by the UK government in 1991. He outlines three reasons for this, the first being that although the Children Act 1989 requires the courts and local authorities, when making decisions concerning a child's upbringing, to give paramount consideration to the welfare of the child, the child's wishes and feelings are only one of several factors to be taken into account in determining this.

However, Adrian James points out that there is no legal requirement on education authorities, schools, health and local authorities, parents, or national government to give consideration to the ascertainable wishes and feelings of children. Consequently, because children have no legal right to be consulted, this allows adult decision-makers to set aside a child's wishes and feelings if the decision-maker feels that these are contrary to the child's long-term interests. He also stresses that since the implementation of the Children Act there has been no review of the legislative changes required to give legal effect to Article 12 of the UNCRC.

James clarifies that although Article 12 contains important caveats concerning the age and maturity of a child, it makes it clear that a child has the right to express his or her views in family proceedings, a right that

Family Court Review, Volume 46, Issue 1, https://onlinelibrary.wiley.com/doi/full/10.1111/j.1744-1617.2007.00183.x

is not contained in the Children Act. Adrian James also explains that a number of influential non-government organisations interested in children and the promotion of their rights, came together as the Children's Rights Alliance for England (CRAE).

This coalition of over 180 member organisations, drawn mainly from the voluntary sector, took a considerable and very public interest in the government's compliance with the UNCRC. He suggests that this created considerable additional pressure for the widespread implementation of the provisions of the UNCRC, particularly in public and state institutions. Although children's views could be set aside in judicial proceedings by means of reference to the welfare of the child and the need to make decisions in their best interests, it was much more difficult to deny children their Article 12 participation rights more generally.

Adrian James concludes:

> It is clear that since the reorganization of the welfare and support services for the family courts with the creation of CAFCASS, there have been significant changes in the environment within which children's issues are addressed in both private and public law cases in the family courts.

And he further states:

> It is also clear that at an organizational level major strides have been taken in embracing the provisions of the UNCRC and in making children's rights, especially those of participation, meaningful. At the level of both judicial and child welfare practice, however, progress has been more patchy in the areas of practice in which individual adult attitudes and values in relation to children and childhood are more difficult to influence and change.

The Joint Committee on Human Rights

Although rather beyond the primary scope for this book, it is worth mentioning that in 2009 the Joint Committee on Human Rights (JCHR) published its report on children's rights and recommended that further information be given by the UK government about the extent to which UNCRC rights are or are not already protected by UK law.

The government response in 2010[9] was prepared by the specialist Children's Rights and Participation Team at the Department for Children

---

[9] IMPLEMENTATION OF THE UNCRC IN ENGLAND – MAPPING EXERCISE (publishing.service.gov.uk) The United Nations Convention on the Rights of the Child: How legislation underpins implementation in England Further information for the Joint Committee on Human Rights March 2010 Work in progress, Children's Rights and Participation Team Department for Children, Schools and Families, Ground Floor, 20 Great Smith Street, London

Schools and Families. It set out how 'implementation of the convention is achieved through a substantial body of legislation and by putting the UNCRC at the heart of policies for children and young people'.

It also explains: 'The document demonstrates how England complies with each article in the UNCRC through our legislation and case law, administration and other processes.' It then adds that it is not an exhaustive list of all of those who are relevant in considering the convention articles, although the key provisions are included. These demonstrate how the rights and obligations set out in the UNCRC are protected in England.

The Human Rights Act 1998

The Human Rights Act 1998, which came into force in October 2000, has significant implications for family law and Cafcass. It provides for the first time for the enforcement of the European Convention on Human Rights against a public authority directly through to any level of the domestic courts. Over time it would require Cafcass practitioners to take the Act carefully into account in close coordination with the family judiciary and other key professionals. Hopefully, there are other accounts dealing with the interface between the Human Rights Act and Cafcass for any readers who may wish to explore this issue in greater depth.

Article 8 (Right to Respect for Private and Family Life) states:

> 1. Everyone has the right to respect for his private and family life, his home and his correspondence.
>
> 2. There shall be no interference by a public authority with the exercise of this right except such as in accordance with the law and is necessary in a democratic society in the interests of national security, public safety or the economic well-being of the country, for the prevention of disorder or crime, for the protection of health or morals, or for the protection of the rights and freedoms of others.

Leonie Jordan, a member of Cafcass' first board, recollects:

> *The first chief executive appointed came from a probation background with, it seemed, limited understanding of the role of the children's guardian – both the history of this role and the centrality of their independence together with the tandem model in representing the child in the court process and having regard to the child's Article 8 rights.*

And writing in 2001, I recall:

Attending a seminar for senior civil servants held at the Lord Chancellor's Department around the time of the Act's implementation. It was addressed with clarity and humour by Professor Brenda Hoggett.

The Children Act 2004

The Act,[10] of which different parts came into force on different dates, established the Children's Commissioner for England.[11] The accompanying explanatory notes[12] set out the background in the following way:

> In September 2003, the Government published the Every Child Matters Green Paper alongside its formal response[13] to the Victoria Climbié Inquiry Report'[14] The Green Paper proposed changes in policy and legislation in England to maximise opportunities and minimise risks for all children and young people, focusing services more effectively around the needs of children, young people and families.
>
> The consultation on the Green Paper showed broad support for the proposals, in particular the intention to concentrate on outcomes that children and young people themselves have said are important, rather than prescribing organisational change. The Act has been produced in the light of this consultation and gives effect to the legislative proposals set out in the Green Paper to create clear accountability for children's services, to enable better joint working and to secure a better focus on safeguarding children. Alongside the Act, the Government has published Every Child Matters: Next Steps. This provides details of the consultation response and the wider, non-legislative, elements of change that are being taken forward to promote the well-being of all children.
>
> To ensure a voice for children and young people at national level ... the Act provides for the establishment of a Children's Commissioner ... the Commissioner's role will be to promote awareness of the views and interests of children (and certain groups of vulnerable young adults) in England. The Commissioner will also be able to hold inquiries – on direction by the Secretary of State or on his own initiative – into cases of individual children with wider policy relevance in England or, on non-devolved matters, in other parts of the UK.

---

[10] Children Act 2004 (legislation.gov.uk)

[11] https://www.childrenscommissioner.gov.uk/

[12] https://www.legislation.gov.uk/ukpga/2004/31/notes/contents

[13] https://assets.publishing.service.gov.uk/media/5a7ef0c440f0b6230268c7e4/Victoria_Climbie_inquiry_report_-_Governments_response.pdf

[14] https://assets.publishing.service.gov.uk/media/5a7c5edeed915d696ccfc51b/5730.pdf

Readers will be aware that the subject of both children's rights and human rights continues to attract media and political attention, although often from opposing viewpoints.

9

Family Justice Developments

This chapter considers some significant events about family justice and new approaches to dealing with certain care-related proceedings. The development of government policy around domestic violence is explored from a Department of Health perspective. The 2011 Justice Committee and Family Justice Review reports, together with their respective government responses, are also covered, as are examples of more recent reports about aspects of the family justice system.

A Devon Conference

Interdisciplinary working around family law proceedings took a significant step with a Devon conference held in September 1995 for judges, psychiatrists and other professionals concerned with the protection of children within the family justice system. I attended from the Department of Health, which together with the Judicial Studies Board helped fund the event. The papers were later published.[1]

In its foreword, Lord Lloyd of Berwick wrote:

> Dartington Hall has played host to many such conferences in the past. What made this conference unique was the attendance of so many judges coming to discuss with mental health professionals the almost insoluble problems which they face every day in court.

The conference led to the formation of the President's Interdisciplinary Committee, which held its first meeting on 30 April 1996 in the President's Chambers at the Royal Courts of Justice in London and was chaired by the then president of the Family Division, Sir Stephen Brown. I was a member of the committee while working at the Department of Health.

Its successor body, as noted in an earlier chapter, was the Family Justice Council (FJC), which was established following a consultation published in March 2002 by the then titled Lord Chancellor's Department. It proposed the establishment of a committee to promote interdisciplinary cooperation and best practice and to advise the government on issues

[1] *Rooted Sorrows: Psychoanalytic Perspectives on Child Protection Assessment, Therapy and Treatment*, Family Law, 1997

affecting the family justice system. The proposal was widely supported, and the establishment of the FJC was approved by the Lord Chancellor in May 2003. The FJC became operational in July 2004. It is a non-statutory advisory body that monitors the effectiveness of the family justice system and advises on reforms necessary for continuous improvement. Its activities are also publicised via its website.[2]

The President's Interdisciplinary Committee Conference

Wardship

Prior to the Children Act 1989, many local authorities relied extensively on the wardship[3] provisions for a range of reasons, but section 100 of the Act significantly restricted this avenue by repealing section 7 of the Family Law Act 1969. Some of the family judiciary regretted this change, considering, at its simplest, that the court should retain a reviewing power over the actions of local authorities when the latter are charged with implementing the care plan pursuant to a care order. This situation is usefully summarised by Lord Justice Thorpe in the Court of Appeal judgment[4] also referred to later and some of which is quoted below:

> Although the powers of the Family Division judge in wardship were limited, particularly after the decision of the House of Lords in *A v Liverpool City Council* [1982] AC 363, one of the undoubted characteristics of that regime was the ability of the local authority to share with the judge the responsibility for decisions that were either agonisingly difficult or that would be acutely painful to the parents. Having practised through that era both as an advocate and as a judge of the Division, I am in no doubt that there were many authorities which in many cases found the availability of the judge as the decision maker supportive not only at the point of trial but also in the subsequent implementation of the judgment reached at trial. The radical departure introduced by the Children Act 1989, whilst based on very sound policy considerations, required a major adjustment to be made not only by judges but also local authorities, guardians ad litem and forensic experts. As these groups grew used to working with the new tool, there is no doubt that the general reception was one of profound appreciation.

Family Justice Council - Courts and Tribunals Judiciary

Wards of Court, Lowe, N. V. and White R. A. H., Butterworths, 1979

W & Ors (Children), Re [2001] EWCA Civ 757 (23 May 2001) (bailii.org) paragraph 18

1997 Conferences

I had also discussed some of these care-related issues at the President's Conference for the Designated Family Judges held in May 1997. While there, I wrote:[5]

> Having an earnest early morning conversation with Dame Elizabeth Butler-Sloss, where we reached an agreement 'in principle' – after which we left the swimming pool and joined the others for breakfast.

The theme for the next two-day residential conference held in September 1997 was 'Care Planning Within the Family Justice System'. It was again part funded by the Department of Health, and I helped plan its programme with Lord Justice Mathew Thorpe, Tess Duncan, panel manager for Surrey, and Peter Harris, the Official Solicitor. Its main theme was chosen in part because care-planning issues had been causing concerns to judges, local authorities and guardians, and also in the Department of Health.

My paper at the September conference, which I shared with Rupert Hughes to gain his support, was among the 10 that were all published later.[6] The themes I addressed were:

- how care planning policy developed within the Department of Health;
- what local authority front line staff said about care plans made in the first six months of 1995;
- how a range of judiciary reported their experiences in using plans in proceedings;
- whether the care plan guidance issued by the Department of Health in 1991 is still helpful;
- whether involvement of the courts might improve practice and whether oversight of care plan implementation is a possibility in terms of revised policy.

But I also sought to clarify:

> Lastly, may I emphasise that as far as possible a clear distinction is made (and intended) between descriptions of official department policy and other ideas in this paper which are not official policy.

Prior to the conference, I wrote to the head of Family Policy at the Lord Chancellor's Department about my intended paper with a simila

---

[5] Op. cit. 6

[6] *Divided Duties*, Family Law, 1998

clarification. That this caution was not carefully noted in some quarters led to some later problems.

In my paper to the September 1997 Divided Duties conference, I said:

> Of course, what is fundamental is whether the policy which lay behind section 100 and the decisive cut-off point at the making of a care order should in any way be disturbed. Before any change in policy were to be proposed, more detailed thinking is needed.

I then listed eight example questions and explained that some of these points had been discussed earlier that year by a number of Family Division judges who unsurprisingly favoured a post-care order review. As suggested at that conference, Her Honour Judge Valerie Pearlman and I had further discussions a few weeks later and mapped out a possible procedure for a care-plan review. The suggestions arising from these discussions were summarised under nine headings:

> Threshold criteria; Timetable; Bringing the application; Review power; Repeat applications; Notifying the guardian; Reports for review hearing; Involving the parents; Other family proceedings applications.

In my paper, I noted that the Adoption Bill, which was published as a consultative document in 1996, included a clause that dealt with care plans. This proposed a new sub-section to the Children Act that said no care order may be made with respect of a child until the court has considered a plan for the future care of the child. It also made it mandatory for the local authority to prepare a care plan within a timetable set down by the court. It required the local authority to keep the plan under review and, if some change was necessary, to revise it or make a new plan. The plan must give any prescribed information and do so in the prescribed manner. But as noted later, this proposal did not become law.

My comments also suggested:

> This paper is essentially about improved practices by local authorities whilst at the same time questioning whether some of the fundamental responsibilities of courts, local authorities and guardians might need to be realigned. There are issues about power and control – who has how much – and whether it is exercised in a way which promotes the welfare of children.

Finally, drawing on Joan Hunt's distinguished research,[7] I emphasised:

'The Best Laid Plans: Outcomes of Judicial Decisions in Child Protection Cases', Ed Hunt J, DoH, 1999

> Care orders are, by and large, only made in the most difficult and worrying of cases. Instant cures do not exist – for some children the best achievable outcome might be little more than the so-called 'damage limitation exercise'. Predicting what course of action will best promote the welfare of children remains hugely difficult for the courts themselves, but also for those in a professional and advisory role in the court proceedings. This is not an exact science and decision-making therefore needs to be approached with great care and, frankly, a substantial degree of humility. Sound assessments and planning be of fundamental importance.

There were just over 60 attendees at the conference and most knew and respected each other and were at the top of their respective professions. Discussions were frank, constructive and friendly. However, there was an exception as I recall:[8]

> *Playing croquet with Rupert Hughes against Mrs Justice Brenda Hale and one of her fellow judges that revealed a streak of unsuspected aggression and tactical guile – and the Department of Health was roundly defeated.*

When concluded, the discussions at the September conference did not suggest any change in the law, but they did urge improvements in care-planning processes, of which one example was the later Department of Health's Local Authority Circular LAC (99)29. Further details about it are given below.

Care-planning Study

The 1998 Social Services Inspectorate (SSI) study,[9] on which I led, also dealt with some of the same care-planning issues that had been discussed at the 1997 conferences. The study report had three hoped-for outcomes, which were:

- an analysis of care plans to establish what proportion were altered to a significant degree
- proposals for good practice within local authorities and in communication with courts when significant changes in care plans are needed
- a model in respect of format and content of care plans which might have assisted in any implementation of clause 87 of the Adoption

[8] Op. cit. 6

[9] 'Care Planning and Court Orders; Monitoring the Children Act 1989 – Court Order Study', Department of Health, 1998

Bill (published in April 1996) but subsequently not included to date in the government's legislative programme

The study also outlined the history and current concerns:

> Prior to the implementation of the Children Act, there was no requirement that in seeking a care order from the court, local authorities should set out their proposals for the child's future. But beyond being satisfied that the 'threshold criteria' for making an order existed section 1(5) restricted courts by directing that they should only make an order if doing so was better for the child than making no order.
>
> The Act and its subordinate legislation make no reference to care plans although a section in the court application form for a care order requests a plan for the child or children (Form C13). Instead, these considerations are left to the guidance issues in 1991 which developed an outline framework for planning the care of every child looked after by local authorities. This local authority planning tool took on increasing importance in court settings and judgments stressed its significance and the duty of the court to scrutinise plans.

The study explained that where local authorities have altered care plans, sometimes significantly, courts have felt their intentions have been thwarted. This has led to a certain level of mistrust between courts and the local authorities. These kinds of issues were reported in the Children Act Advisory Committee's Annual Report 1994–95[10] and in Dame Margaret Booth's Second Report,[11] where she wrote:

> One local authority commented that there were three different approaches to what a care plan should contain, those of the local authority, of the guardian ad litem and of the court.

The final outcome was that the Adoption Bill was never included in the government's legislative programme before the 1997 general election. Instead, I wrote a local authority circular which was first circulated in draft for consultation. Later it was issued as statutory guidance in 1999.[12,13] The circular reiterates the concerns discussed above; covers 15 areas of practice and policy; and refers to many of the reports also mentioned above. It then advises on the content of a care plan within a five-sections format:

---

[10] Op. cit. 159, pages 36–37

[11] 'Avoiding Delay in Public Law Children Act Cases', Local Government Chronicle, February 1996

[12] 'Care Plans and Care Proceedings under the Children Act 1989', LAC (99)29, DoH, August 1999

[13] [ARCHIVED CONTENT] (nationalarchives.gov.uk)

- Overall aim
- Child's needs, including contact
- Views of others
- Placement detail and timetable
- Management and support by local authority

Within these are included 24 elements mainly based on the Children Act guidance published in 1991. The circular also provides further guidance about the format of care plans, applications involving siblings, endorsement of the plan within the local authority and reviewing the implementation of the care plan.

The Western Circuit Conference

Again organised and chaired by Senior Judge, James Holman, in autumn 2000, I was once more invited by him to speak at Dartington Hall on day two about current Department of Health issues. Cafcass was invited to speak on day one. I wrote at that time:[14]

> A few days before the conference, James Holman rang me to say that Cafcass had let him down and could not come as they had not noted it in their diaries. I commiserated and said I was in Norwich all day on the Monday but, tough as it might be on the audience, I was prepared to speak twice on Tuesday ... James was extremely grateful. Unfortunately, my commitments at the University of East Angia and then as a guest speaker at the AGM of a contact centre in Norwich meant that my delayed train did not reach London until 11.30. After a short night in a Paddington hotel, I caught the 6.30 train to Newton Abbott. From there an elderly lady drove her taxi like the proverbial 'bat out of hell' on wet and twisty roads and I reached Dartington just as James was in the middle of his introductory remarks. I gave one paper in the morning and another in the afternoon. I also accepted his kind gift of a bottle of champagne before sharing with him a convivial train journey from Totnes back to London.

The House of Lords Judgment

Leaving the Department of Health in January 2001 after nearly 16 years was a much greater wrench that I had anticipated. I wrote of that time:[15]

> It was in part the severance from close and respected colleagues. But it was also that I felt that no one was going to replace me at the department or would know the history which was such an important part of my job. Both

---

[14] Op. cit. 6

[15] Op. cit. 6

> predictions proved entirely right. The latter was brought into sharp focus when I was telephoned urgently by former colleagues in early March. They were in the middle of a High Court Appeal. It was about care planning and also involved questions under the Human Rights Act that were aimed at challenging the finality of the making of a care order.
>
> The appeal judges, being family experts, had referred to the September 1997 Highgate House conference and its report *Divided Duties* which two of them had attended. No one in the Department of Health or the Lord Chancellor's Department knew of it – less than four years previously. I jumped into a taxi from my Millbank Tower office with a copy of the report for counsel's use first thing the next day.

The Court of Appeal case led to a significant judgment in the House of Lords[16]on 14 March 2002.

The 'starred' care-order approach was taken forward as a 'judicial initiative', as the House of Lords judgment[17] explains in its opening paragraph:

> These appeals concern the impact of the Human Rights Act 1998 on Parts III and IV of the Children Act 1989. The Court of Appeal[18] (Thorpe, Sedley and Hale LJ) made, in the words of Thorpe LJ, two major adjustments and innovations in the construction and application of the Children Act. The principal issue before your Lordships' House concerns the soundness of this judicial initiative.

The judgment at over 100 paragraphs provides a valuable overview, as does the Re W Court of Appeal case. The former rightly ended the 'starred' care order review ideas which, of course, had never been the official policy of either the Department of Health or the Lord Chancellor's Department, although it had been creatively 'borrowed' by some senior members of the judiciary as if it was.

Following these conferences, reports, research, guidance, Court of Appeal cases and the House of Lords appeal discussed above, section 15 of the Children and Families Act 2014 eventually made statutory arrangements that require care plans to be produced at court when local authorities seek a care order under section 31 of the Children Act 1989.

---

[16] House of Lords - In Re S (FC) In Re S and Others In Re W and Others (First Appeal)(FC) In Re W and Others (Second Appeal) (Conjoined Appeals) (parliament.uk)

[17] Ibid.

[18] W & Ors (Children), Re [2001] EWCA Civ 757 (23 May 2001) (bailii.org)

Changes at the Department of Health

Significant senior management changes in the Department of Health started in 1996 with the retirement of Rupert Hughes and shortly after, another 'downsizing exercise' across government, with 20% cuts at least demanded. In the Department of Health, numerous staff left or were offered early retirement.

Writing of that period in 2001, I said:[19]

> This whole exercise was disastrous because there was no proper analysis of the department's needs to conduct its work. The wrong people were allowed to leave and, utterly predicably, there was an urgent need to recruit again within a year. Why did it happen? In the Thatcher years, professionals were badly undermined and downgraded ... we were seen as too powerful in pushing forward a huge child care agenda ... the department took its revenge.

The Headquarters SSI Child Care Group was abolished. Some transferred to other government departments; others took early retirement. And so ended a significant period of history covering important aspects of relationships between central government, local authorities, the family judiciary, the voluntary sector and the research community, of which more detail is given in Chapter 10.

Wendy Rose

Heading the SSI Child Care Group at the Department of Health before the departmental 'downsizing', Wendy Rose's contribution to the development of child care policies and practice, both before and after the Children Act 1989 was implemented, was of great significance. Her enforced departure was a classic departmental 'own goal', deeply regretted not only by her immediate colleagues but also by many from much further afield.

Wendy Rose's enthusiasm and leadership were matched with hard work and professionalism. Her great sense of vision was accompanied by a necessary sense of humour. She was an excellent public speaker. Her accompanying overhead projector slides and/or flip charts always demonstrated the highest standards of calligraphy.

---

[19] Op. cit. 6

Domestic Violence

One consequence of these departmental changes was that I was 'invited' to take over the policy lead of the branch that included domestic violence within its remit. The Home Office had overall policy responsibility across government for domestic violence. For some years there had been an interdepartmental group and a ministerial group, with officials attending from all over the country. I attended some of these meetings and had doubts about their effectiveness. With a new government after the May 1997 general election, there was a chance to give this subject a higher profile.

Writing in 2001, I said:[20]

> Ministers were keen to start a new publicity/awareness campaign. Paul Boateng wanted to press ahead quickly with a DH one and indeed a good deal of money had already been spent in working up proposals. Other ministers did not want DH to go ahead and felt that everyone should await the new campaign even though, as predicted, under the title Breaking the Chain it took another 18 months to be launched. Mr Boateng would not back down but had to do so shortly after when he was advised that the company we were using had run into financial irregularity claims and adverse media comment.

One part of my role was to help voluntary organisations with their draft section 64 grant applications to the department for ministerial approval for funding,[21] although applications exceeded by a factor of three the money available. I also wrote of that time:[22]

> Domestic violence is a major health issue and costs the NHS huge amounts of money. Many NHS employees are also victims of violence. The NHS executive with whom I worked was reluctant to issue guidelines and preferred to leave it to the professional bodies representing nurses, doctors, consultants and other groups. I felt a more coordinated lead and collaboration was needed and this did begin to happen.

Part IV of the Act (Family Homes and Domestic Violence) was due to be implemented in October 1997 and also covered non-molestation orders and some of the consequential amendments to the emergency protection provisions in the Children Act 1989. The Department of Health circular had to explain what domestic violence is, as well as the law, the

20 Op. cit. 6

21 https://www.legislation.gov.uk/ukpga/1968/46/section/64/enacted

22 Op. cit. 6

background, the changes to court rules and some of the implications for professional practice for groups like local authority social workers and guardians ad litem.

Writing in 2001, I said:[23]

> I drafted the circular, together with a number of annexes, in a short period of time and sought comments from my Lord Chancellor's Department colleagues as they had the policy lead on the Act. I also shared copies with researchers in the field, the judiciary and the head of Women's Aid. As a result, the circular when finalised was quite highly regarded. I remained of the opinion that however simply I set them out in the circular including the use of coloured text boxes, the legal provisions were too complex to be readily understood by busy practitioners.

Other government departments, such as the Department of the Environment, Transport and the Regions (DETR), with its housing responsibilities and, therefore, the lead on homelessness and refuges, had an impressive research programme. I attended its advisory group. The Women's Unit did its best to coordinate all government departments' efforts, and in June 1999 it published Living Without Fear as the government's strategy for tacking domestic violence.

Commissioning a comprehensive training pack funded by the Department of Health was crucial, and I explain:[24]

> I obtained the money and invited bids from likely organisations and all three contenders gave excellent presentations … we could easily have chosen any of the three but decided on a group led by the NSPCC and involving Barnardo's and Bristol University. One led on writing the comprehensive reader; another on the training pack; and the third on the production side.

Making an Impact – Children and Domestic Violence was published in 1998. I chaired the steering group. In the preface to the reader, I wrote:

> It is mainly women who experience domestic violence and it is largely men who perpetrate such violence. But children are frequently caught in the middle. They often witness the violence directly or they are aware that it is happening in the home. As a result, they may be damaged both emotionally and physically … The publication of the training pack … comes at an important time. During its first year in office, the new government has repeatedly stressed its determination to tackle domestic violence urgently and comprehensively. Across government there are a number of departments with vital roles to play

[23] Op. cit. 6

[24] Op. cit. 6

> in the development of strategic policies. These need drawing together to ensure an integrated and complete picture. The practical effects of the new legal framework provided by Part IV of the Family Law Act 1996 which was implemented in the autumn of 1997 are beginning to emerge.

The Adoption and Children Act

The Adoption and Children Act 2002 included an important domestic-violence-related amendment to section 31(9) of the 1989 Children Act that deals with the grounds for making care and supervision orders – namely:

> (2) A court may only make a care order or supervision order if it is satisfied—
> (a) that the child concerned is suffering, or is likely to suffer, significant harm; and
> (b) that the harm, or likelihood of harm, is attributable to—
> (i) the care given to the child, or likely to be given to him if the order were not made, not being what it would be reasonable to expect a parent to give to him; or
> (ii) the child's being beyond parental control.
>
> . . . . .
>
> (9) In this section—
> 'harm' means ill-treatment or the impairment of health or development including, for example, impairment suffered from seeing or hearing the ill-treatment of another.

The Family Law Act

A parliamentary debate on the Family Law Act on 4 April 2000 summarises a wide range of key issues about this proposed legislation,[25] as does a 2019 House of Commons Library briefing paper.[26] The then Secretary of State Mrs Virginia Bottomley's opening remarks begin:

> I address the House on an issue that affects many families and children. Divorce is a deeply painful experience for the couple, their children, their parents, their family, their friends and the taxpayer. The recent Economic and Social Research Council document 'Family and Household Change in Britain' by Alison Wertheimer and Susan McRae says that, with more than 40 per cent. of marriages ending in divorce, the increase in marital breakdown in Britain is a major political and social concern. Britain heads the European league table. There were 145,200 divorces in the United Kingdom in 1998. It is mildly encouraging that the figure is lower than it was in 1991, but it remains an enormously important issue.

5 https://api.parliament.uk/historic-hansard/commons/2000/apr/04/family-law-act-1996

6 https://researchbriefings.files.parliament.uk/documents/SN01409/SN01409.pdf

> Divorce is a particularly important issue when children are involved. It scars the lives of many. Children and their families suffer alike if there are on-going resentments, arguments and distress. Through my work as the chairman of a juvenile court for many years, a researcher into child poverty and an executive member of the Children's Society, as well as my work as a Member of Parliament and a Minister, I have long witnessed first-hand the pain and suffering that divorce can cause.

Representation of Children's Views in Private Law Proceedings

The Joseph Rowntree-funded research report in 2000[27] discusses the situation regarding the representation of children's views in private law proceedings, how these views could be better represented under new arrangements, and children's views as expressed to researchers.

This wide-ranging report included a section drawn from a seminar for members of the Lord Chancellor's Advisory Board on Family Law held on 5 July 1999. I was the Department of Health 'observer' member. The purpose of the report was to summarise the findings of current research on the issues of listening to children and considering their best interests. This was in the context of the development of court rules in relation to Part II of the Family Law Act 1996 (FLA), which proposed amendments to the grounds for granting a divorce or separation.

The report summarised the findings of research on 'the present situation regarding the representation of children's views in private law proceedings, the more effective representation of children's views under new arrangements, and children's views on how they would like to be involved'.

However, shortly before the July seminar, the Lord Chancellor announced on 17 June 1999 that the enactment of Part II of the FLA would be postponed. This Part provides for compulsory attendance at an information meeting before a statement of marital breakdown is filed, and a period of reflection. The preliminary research results from the information meetings were viewed by the Lord Chancellor as disappointing.

I wrote:[28]

> Members of the advisory committee were upset and some were so angry that they wanted to resign immediately. Although technically as an 'observer' I should not have been allowed to speak, the chairman allowed my request

[27] https://www.jrf.org.uk/sites/default/files/jrf/migrated/files/1859353363.pdf

[28] Op. cit. 6

to do so. I stressed that the committee's title included the word 'advisory', and sometimes advice, however well meant, was not taken by ministers. Whatever their deeply hurt feelings, I urged them not to resign and argued that countless couples going through divorce around the country needed their ongoing help. My words seemingly struck home as nobody resigned.

The Lord Chancellor's decision meant that there was no longer an immediate concern with developing associated court rules, and therefore the discussion at the July seminar was more broad-ranging, touching on general problems to do with changing the wider cultural setting as well as specific points regarding the court welfare service. *The Guardian* reported the Lord Chancellor's decision the following day.[29]

Sir Nicholas Wall

Sir Nicholas Wall was president of the Family Division from 2010 until 2015. He delivered a paper in September 2010 titled 'Is the Family Justice System in Need of Review?'[30] to a conference organised by the campaigning charity Families Need Fathers. It was typical that he would not shy away from addressing what might have been a highly critical audience. His opening comments set the tone for discussing important issues around private law:

> 1. As phrased there can, of course, be only one answer to the question posed as the title to this paper. No system is immune from the need for review. I have no doubt that there would be those both within and without who would say that Families Need Fathers is in need of review. The art is realistically to recognise both the weaknesses and the strengths of any institution: to build on the latter and to improve the former. Very few organisations are wholly good or wholly bad, and the Family Justice System is no exception.
>
> 2. The best thing about the Family Justice System, in my view, is the people who work in it. Most of them, in my experience, are decent, honest and hardworking. They are not in it for the money, but do the work because they believe in it. This may not be a view you share. You may tell me that your experience is different. But it is always a mistake, I think, automatically to attack the good faith of the professionals with whom you deal. If they go wrong, they need to be told, and will be told. I could easily spend the rest of this paper giving you examples of the occasions in which I have been critical of circuit judges, social workers and CAFCASS officers.

---

[29] https://www.theguardian.com/politics/1999/jun/18/uk.politicalnews4

[30] https://www.judiciary.uk/wp-content/uploads/JCO/Documents/Speeches/pfd-speech-families-need-fathers-19092010.pdf

3. The impression I have gained so far is that the government is likely to invest heavily in the outcome of the Family Justice Review currently underway. Be under no illusions. The recommendations are likely to be radical. There are no sacred cows. I have no idea what the final recommendations will be, but you do not need a crystal ball to see that legal aid for private law proceedings is likely to be further diminished if not abolished: that long and protracted contact and residence disputes will become things of the past, and that out of court mediation and conciliation will be encouraged.

4. I propose this morning to identify and to address three specific areas in which the Family Justice System has been criticised. They are (1) shared residence and contact; (2) Payne v Payne; (3) McKenzie friends. All three are, I think, relevant to what you think and do. But before I turn to each in turn, I need to make some preliminary points.

5. It does not take much thought to realise how the adversarial system permeates our national life. Parliament is based on it. There is government and opposition. Debates are conducted by means of proposition and opposition. Cases are described as X against Y. Newspapers thrive on it. Black is black and white is white. Something is nearly always somebody's fault. I could easily multiply examples.

And later he continues:

13. Family law does not fit easily into either concept. Separating parents rarely behave reasonably, although they always believe that they are doing so, and that the other party is behaving unreasonably. If both parties are acting reasonably, they usually do not need a court to resolve their differences.

14. In addition, the Family Justice System has been grafted on to the common law. One party wants a divorce, or residence or contact: the other opposes it. One party makes an application, the other resists. The adversarial system is engrained.

15. The first and critical change which, therefore, needs to be made is to make the system less adversarial. This is not as easy as it sounds. Issue of fact arise which have to be resolved (particularly where domestic abuse is alleged.) Furthermore, disputes over contact between absent parents and their former partners (married or otherwise) are rarely about the children concerned. Far more often, the parties are fighting over again the battles of the relationship, and the children are both the battlefield and the ammunition. Often the mother, who finds herself caring for the children, is able to use her power over them to deny the father contact. It is very easy for one party to say that he or she is acting in the best interests of the child concerned, and

> that the other party is not; it is quite another to understand that both think they are and often that neither is.

Sir Nicholas was another senior judge with whom I had a close working relationship. Although not for professional reasons, this continued especially after his enforced retirement brought on by ill- health and continued up to the week of his death in 2017. The Guardian obituary was written by Dame Elizabeth Butler-Sloss.[31]

> The illness that led the judge Sir Nicholas Wall to take his own life at the age of 71 had consequences beyond the profound loss felt by his family, friends and the legal community. Though a diagnosis of a rare form of dementia came only recently, he had retired as president of the family division at the onset of the condition in 2012. This deprived the family courts and the wider world of a leading exponent of this field of law at a moment when his innovative plans had not yet come fully into effect.

The Family Drug and Alcohol Court

Probably the most significant change in policy and practice with regard to some care-related proceedings and with implications for Cafcass has been the well-researched but slowly scaled up family drug and alcohol court (FDAC). This was first pioneered as a pilot in 2008 by District Judge Nicholas Crichton at the Inner London Family Proceedings Court[32] who died in 2018.[33] It was initially evaluated by a research team at Brunel University primarily funded by the Nuffield Foundation. It has been adapted to English law and practice from a model of family treatment drug courts (FTDCs) that is widely used in the USA. A briefing paper from the research team drawn from a longer report[34] states:

> The catalysts for the UK pilot were the encouraging evidence from the US evaluation and the concerns about the response to parental substance misuse through ordinary care proceedings in England. These concerns were about the poor child and parent outcomes; insufficient co-ordination between adult and children's services; late intervention to protect children; delay in reaching decisions; and the soaring costs of proceedings, linked to the length of proceedings and the cost of expert evidence.

---

[1] https://www.theguardian.com/law/2017/mar/01/sir-nicholas-wall-obituary
[2] https://bura.brunel.ac.uk/handle/2438/5909
[3] https://www.theguardian.com/law/2018/dec/21/nicholas-crichton-obituary
[4] *Changing Lifestyles, Keeping Children Safe: An evaluation of the first Family Drug and Alcohol Court (FDAC) in care proceedings,* Harwin, J., Alrouh, B., Ryan, M. and Tunnard J., Brunel University, London

The FDAC model is therapeutic problem-solving replacing standard care proceedings for those parents who agree to participate. FDACs are courts for parents whose children are subject to proceedings due to their drug and alcohol problems. The model is designed to enable parents to stop misusing drugs and alcohol so that, where possible, children can remain with their families. Practitioners and judiciary work from the belief that all parents can change and should be given the support to do so, as well as an understanding that much change is achieved through, and in, trusting relationships.

The approach, therefore, seeks to reduce the adversarial and punitive elements of proceedings and introduce a collaborative model. FDACs use a problem-solving court approach, which means that the judge not only adjudicates the case but plays a proactive role in motivating parents. This is achieved through judicial continuity and judicial monitoring, as well as a focus on the relational power of the judge as an agent for change.[35]

A later evaluation of the FDAC, *Implications for Policy and Practice,* was published in 2023.[36] The study recommends that the Department for Education should consider 'embedding evaluation, including cost analysis, in any scale-up of problem-solving approaches in family courts'.

A 2009 Celebration

On 28 April 2009 I attended a celebratory event in London organised by Nagalro and marking 25 years of the Guardian Service. Judith Timms OBE, drawing on her deep knowledge of the issues, delivered a historical overview lecture.[37] She reminded her audience that:

> The thorny issue, however, is to reconcile the tension inherent in the need to maintain the independence of professional opinion, whilst at the same time maintaining the dual accountability to both CAFCASS and the courts. Guardians appear before the court and are personally appointed by them as independent expert witnesses in their own right and their professional opinion is sought by the court in that capacity. The role dictates that it may not be subsumed within a line management structure. At the same time CAFCASS is responsible to Government for the overall management and standards of service delivery. This has led to difficulties, particularly for those who are self- employed but also for those who are employed Family Court

[35] https://justiceinnovation.org/project/family-drug-and-alcohol-court-fdac

[36] *Seen and Heard,* Volume 23, Issue 4, pp 28–29

[37] https://www.nagalro.com/_userfiles/pages/files/25_years_of_guardians_where_next_presentation_by_j_timms_obe.pdf

Advisers (FCAs). The 'value added' of the Guardian's input lies not in merely being another report to set alongside the local authority's but in the independence and clear sightedness of its recommendation, untrammelled by any other consideration beyond the welfare of this particular child at a crisis in their life.

More Concerns about Cafcass

While many hoped that Cafcass after nine years would have made substantial progress, when the organisation was the subject of another select committee examination in 2010[38] by the Public Accounts Committee (Sixth Report: Cafcass's Response to Increased Demand for its Services), the criticism was as severe as in 2003, with concluding comments that include:

> 1. Cafcass, as an organisation, is not fit-for-purpose. Many areas still do not provide a timely service to the courts, and the average time to fully allocate care cases at 27 days, down from 40 days, is still well above what it should be. Cafcass and the Department should report back to the Committee in a year, when we will expect to see that they have completed firm actions and undertaken rigorous monitoring to achieve the large amount of improvement that is still required.

And:

> 10. Cafcass has taken too long to secure essential changes, and much of the responsibility lies with top management. Driving through the Transformation Programme while overseeing consistent improvements in the level of service will take strong and vigorous leadership and communication. The Department should regularly monitor Cafcass's progress in implementing the Programme, holding senior management to account for any delay. Cafcass and the Department should review the robustness of the Programme regularly and take action promptly to resolve emerging problems.

Further Concerns

Another example of Parliament's detailed involvement in examining longstanding Cafcass difficulties is found in the wide-ranging Justice Committee's Sixth Report of Session 2010–12: Operation of the Family Courts,[39] of which only one section focuses on Cafcass.

Both the committee's concerns and the government's response to them are set out below. The extent to which Cafcass was involved in drafting

[38] https://publications.parliament.uk/pa/cm201011/cmselect/cmpubacc/439/43902.htm

[39] Presented to Parliament by the Lord Chancellor and Secretary of State for Justice by command of Her Majesty, October 2011: gov-response-operation-of-the-family-courts.pdf (justice.gov.uk)

any of the government's responses may be a matter for speculation, as also is perhaps the degree to which Cafcass agreed with them.

Committee's Historical Summary

The report's opening sentence of the section on Cafcass' history somewhat understates the position:

> 162. Cafcass was created in 2001 and has had a number of problems since then.

It then continues with much cross-referencing to paragraphs elsewhere in the report:

> In 2003 the Chairman of the Board resigned after a very critical report by our predecessor Committee which called for a fundamental review of its operation. The then Lord Chancellor (who was responsible for the Board at the time) then invited the other Board members to resign. Later, the death of Baby Peter in 2007 and the subsequent increase in the number of care proceedings put the organisation under considerable pressure and led to lengthy delays in allocating guardians to cases and in completing reports. We heard conflicting versions of the history of Cafcass and the extent to which Cafcass was responsible for its recent problems. We were told that the time prior to Cafcass was 'a golden age' while the Interim Report concluded that 'there was no golden age before the creation of Cafcass'.
>
> Baroness Howarth, Chair of Cafcass, described it as a time when 'we had a Rolls-Royce service for some children, [...] and we had hundreds of other children who were never seen'. It has been suggested to us by Cafcass that its recent problems were caused by a 'surge' in cases after the death of Baby Peter, but we were also told by the Interdisciplinary Alliance for Children that this only increased the number of cases to the levels seen in 1998. Finally we were told that 'the current problems faced by Cafcass are both a cause and a symptom of the continuing long delays. The longer a case goes on the more assessments are ordered and the more work the appointed guardian is expected to devote to any one case.'
>
> 163. After the death of Baby Peter and the resulting increase in care applications, the number of cases Cafcass had not allocated to a guardian grew, with over 900 unallocated cases by September 2009. In order to tackle this, Cafcass and the President of the Family Division drew up the President's Interim Guidance. Introduced in October 2009 and originally designed to last for six months, this remained in place until October 2010 when it was replaced with a Joint Agreement which is expected to last to October 2011. The President's Interim Guidance was designed to allow Cafcass to provide a 'safe minimum service', by focusing on safeguarding

> and task focused work, and providing reports on specific issues rather than on general welfare.
>
> 164. The Minister responsible for Cafcass, Tim Loughton MP, told us that he thought some of the criticism of Cafcass was unfair: 'with all the problems there are with Cafcass, we are going through, hopefully, some quite abnormal times at the moment, given the very high increase in workload that Cafcass has been faced with post-Baby Peter from 2008 onwards. [...] It was slightly unfair to judge Cafcass at that precise time.'

Committee's First Concerns and Government's Response

The committee's first concerns, although noting progress, are about Cafcass case allocation and delay:

> While the exact figures are disputed, it is clear that Cafcass has made substantial progress in reducing the number of unallocated and duty allocated cases in public and private law. We welcome this progress and hope that it can be maintained. It continues to be a cause for concern, however, that Cafcass was unable to reassure us that, in the 221 cases allocated to managers, those managers were working actively on all those cases. We call on Cafcass to measure and monitor the amount of work carried out by managers in cases allocated to them in order to ensure that genuine progress is made and that these cases are not simply moved off the unallocated list to make those performance statistics look more acceptable. We expect Cafcass to report back to us on this point at the earliest reasonable opportunity.

To which the government's detailed response states:

> 40. Cafcass regularly monitors the amount of casework being undertaken by all of its staff including, in particular, managers (the latest figures are set out at paragraph 47 below). It is not Cafcass's practice to leave cases unallocated for any longer than the minimum possible length of time. Similarly, it is Cafcass's policy that cases should only be substantially allocated to those staff who are available to undertake the necessary work in a timely way. Duty allocated cases may be held by staff (including managers) where it is not possible, or necessary, to allocate them on a substantive basis.
>
> 41. The definitions of 'unallocated'; 'duty allocated'; and 'allocated' are as follows:
> Unallocated – brand new cases only.
> Duty allocated – cases where Cafcass will both react to incoming information and also take pro-active steps at appropriate points in time to review the status, needs and level of priority of the case.

Allocated – (substantive or fully allocated) cases where the named worker will both react to incoming information and take appropriate pro-active steps and, in addition, will undertake the work that is set out in the case plan, and also in accordance with the court's requests and directions. A substantive allocation includes the production of the case plan and any required reports for the case. A substantive allocation also includes allocation to an appointment of Children's Guardian by the court in s31 care, supervision and other relevant Public Law cases.

42. The Committee expressed concern that a small proportion of cases (currently 0.7% of the total number of open, substantively allocated cases) is allocated to managers. The Government wishes to point out that these cases include those held by managers who have recently been promoted and who have continued to work on their existing cases to ensure that practitioner continuity is maintained. It is also often valuable for managers to retain a small caseload in order to maintain a direct connection with frontline practice. A further small tranche of cases will often be held on a duty basis by managers before being fully allocated to a named practitioner. Managers undertake the triage of these cases, which is an important first step once the case has been received.

Further Committee Concerns and Government Response

The second of the Justice Committee's concerns states:

We share the concerns of the Committee of Public Accounts about the ability of Cafcass to sustain its recent progress given that there is no sign of a future fall in the number of care applications. We are also concerned about the ability of Cafcass to cope with a range of potential future stresses, including any restructuring of itself or of the court system, any additional delays in the court system, and cuts to local authority budgets (which could lead to more poorly prepared cases reaching court).

To which the government's response is:

43. The Government recognises that Cafcass has continued to absorb further significant increases in public law work in particular and that it is changing its working practices further in order to continue to be able to deal with all incoming work. In doing so, it has demonstrated its resilience as an organisation. Nevertheless, the Government accepts that this continuing pressure on resources poses a strategic risk to Cafcass's performance.

44. Both the Government and Cafcass will continue to keep the situation under regular review, and will reappraise it when the final report of the Family Justice Review is available. Cafcass's Chief Executive has quarterly meetings with the Parliamentary Under-Secretary of State for Children and

Families; in addition there are regular meetings between senior Departmental officials and Cafcass. Departmental officials also meet monthly with the Cafcass management team.

45. The Department also receives monthly performance reports from Cafcass demonstrating its performance against the agreed Key Performance Indicators (KPIs) which are:

- KPI 1 (Public Law): 97% of the public law workload should be allocated when taken as a snapshot.
- KPI 2 (Private Law): 97% of the private law workload should be allocated when taken as a snapshot.
- KPI 3 (Safeguarding and promoting welfare): The quality of practice in safeguarding is rated overall as satisfactory or above in more than 97% of cases.
- KPI 4 (Public Law) Cafcass will allocate (on an ongoing, not a duty basis) all care cases by CMC (Case Management Conference), measured as 45 calendar days from application date, in 97% of cases.
- KPI 7 (Private Law): Cafcass should provide at least 97% of private law reports to court within the agreed filing times, for:
    - multiple issue section 7 reports;
    - single issue section 7 reports;
    - risk assessment section 7 reports; and
    - wishes & feelings section 7 reports.

46. Performance against these indicators is published in Cafcass's Annual Report.

The Committee's Management Concerns and Government Response

The Justice Committee also raises other management concerns:

> We are puzzled and concerned by Cafcass's continued aversion to the use of self-employed guardians, especially when the amount it spends on agency social workers has more than doubled in a year. Self-employed guardians are cheaper than agency staff and no more expensive than directly employed staff. At the same time they offer greater flexibility, and their expertise is valued by the judiciary. Cafcass should be making considerably greater use of self-employed staff, particularly in the geographical areas where it has difficulty recruiting. (Paragraph 180).

To which the government response says:

> 47. The majority of self-employed contractors (SECs) are London-based and Cafcass continues to offer work to them. SECs currently hold 1,240 care cases – about 10% of Cafcass's care workload. In other parts of the country where SECs are not available or have not chosen to take on the work offered to them, Cafcass has employed agency staff to help tackle backlogs on a

time-limited basis; this is partly as a result of the additional one-off funding it received from Government during 2010–11. This increased agency spend in 2010–11 will be reduced in 2011–12. However, Cafcass will continue to use a mixed economy of staff, including employed staff, SECs and agency staff, in order to keep pace with demand and maintain its current levels of allocation. It is for Cafcass to determine the most appropriate staffing structure to fulfil its statutory functions, taking account of resource constraints.

48. The Government notes the Committee's concern and agrees that employed staff are best able to undertake the full range of Cafcass work, while other staff are less flexible. For example, agency staff, whose assignments with Cafcass are time-limited, are generally unsuitable to work as children's guardians in care cases, the average duration of which is more than a year. However, self-employed contractors are generally unwilling to deal with short-term pieces of private law casework which are, in numerical terms, by far the most common type of Cafcass case. Proposed changes to the family justice system in the Interim Report will, if implemented, make demands on Cafcass in terms of change management. It will be crucial for management to deliver that change in ways which support the staff (and self-employed and agency workers) to deliver the necessary services for children.

The Justice Committee's next concern is:

The recent experience of Cafcass managing staff, communicating with stakeholders, and the production of the very imperfect draft Operating Manual all indicate that Cafcass management needs urgently to take steps to improve the way they communicate with staff and with others working in the family justice system. (Paragraph 185).

To which the government response states:

49. The Government agrees that careful and measured change management is pivotal to the successful implementation of the changes that may flow from the recommendations of the Family Justice Review. The recently (July 2011) completed MoJ/DfE survey of the impact of the President's Interim Guidance and the September 2010 'Agreement' provided a clear, positive endorsement of the improved level of communications between Cafcass and its partners. A copy of the survey has been published alongside this Government response.

50. The Operating Manual continues to be developed as a draft, which takes full account of the perspectives offered by the Justice Committee (see paragraph 55 below for further information about the Operating Manual). Whilst we recognise the need for Cafcass to be a managed service and for its staff to be supported, the appointment of experienced social workers could justify a lighter touch in management, allowing professional staff more

> discretion about the way they carry out their role than the detailed and process driven Operating Manual would suggest. This is the future for social workers Professor Munro has set out in her report. Cafcass should look at the lessons that it can learn from her report and adopt Professor Munro's proposed approach. (Paragraph 186)
>
> 51. The Government agrees that Cafcass should look closely at the Government's response to the Munro report with a view to applying the steps being taken by Government to its specialist family court social work service, to the fullest extent possible. Cafcass has indicated that it intends to continue its policy of appointing only experienced social workers to Family Court Adviser posts.

The Committee's Views on the Current System and the Case for Change

The Sixth Justice Committee Report's second section is headed 'The Current System and the Case for Change'. Paragraphs 7 to 10 are set out below and examine the family law context in the following way, extensively cross-referencing to evidence submitted to the committee:

> 7. The family justice system sees cases ranging from the relatively amicable separation of a couple to physical, sexual and emotional child abuse. In the most serious cases, a child's life may be at risk. In 2009–10, 36 children were killed by their parents. Research carried out for the Home Office in 2003 found that, between 1995 and 1999, in 80% of all homicides where the victim was an infant under the age of one, the killer was a parent, and in 'virtually all' the remaining 20% the killer was a family member, friend or someone who had care of the infant.
>
> 8. While the assumption may be that a child's life is at risk primarily in cases of severe neglect and abuse, tragically children have been killed by a parent in the aftermath of relationship breakdown. In February 2010, five-year-old Gabrielle Grady was murdered by her father as he drove his car with her and her six-year-old brother inside into the River Avon, following a row with their mother over contact with the children. In August 2010, in Scotland, Theresa Riggi killed her three children who had been the subject of an on-going residence dispute with her estranged husband. She was found guilty of culpable homicide on the grounds of diminished responsibility.
>
> 9. Abuse within a family, including severe neglect and physical, sexual and emotional violence, remains the reality for many children. In March 2010, there were 46,709 children on the child protection register at risk of abuse or neglect. In 2009–10, the British Crime Survey found that 16,864 sexual offences against children under 16 were recorded in England and Wales, 31% of all sexual crimes and 38% of all rapes. Studies indicate that around 80% of such offences take place in the home of the offender or child, and

the vast majority are committed by someone known to the victim, often a family member. In 2009, a study by the NSPCC found that all types of abuse and neglect of children were under-reported.

10. Violence between adults has been found to have a long-term negative effect on the emotional well-being of children, particularly their ability to form healthy relationships in adult life. Quantifying the incidence of domestic violence is notoriously difficult. In 2008–09 the British Crime Survey found that 42% of victims of all violent offences reported the incident to police, compared with only 16% of domestic violence victims. However, the most reliable figures, from the British Crime Survey, found that 1.2 million adults (780,000 women and 463,000 men) had been the victim of domestic violence in 2008–09, around 4.4% of women and 2.7% of men in the UK. A 2004 survey found 45% of women and 26% of men had reported experiencing at least one incident of domestic violence in their lifetimes. In 2009, some 24,865 non-molestation or occupation orders were made in the county court to protect victims of domestic violence. Studies show that intra-familial violence occurs throughout society, in all social classes and across racial, religious and ethnic groups. Many victims experience repeated attacks, including sexual, physical and emotional abuse: a 2004 survey found that no other crime has such a high repeat victimisation rate. In 2001, the British Crime Survey found that 45% of rape victims were assaulted by current husbands or partners and 9% by former partners. Of the 3,249 women and 6,808 men murdered between 1995 and 2009, 47% and 12% respectively were killed by a partner or ex-partner.

The Committee's View of Data Collection

In offering an overview of the current system, the Justice Committee also highlights the challenges of data collection and analysis:

11. Our primary difficulty throughout this inquiry has been to form a clear picture of trends and changes in the family justice system. The family justice system consists of private law cases, which deal with the consequences of relationship breakdown, and public law cases, which involve child protection. The Ministry of Justice's (MoJ) Judicial and Court Statistics for 2009 tell us that there were 163,290 court cases involving children in England and Wales, 137,480 in private law and 25,810 in public law.

And:

We have heard from many witnesses that the numbers of cases in both public and private law is rising, and this is corroborated by the Ministry of Justice's figures. However, it is impossible for us to gauge the level of that increase given the flaws in compiling the data. The Ministry of Justice's Judicial and

> Court Statistics bulletin for 2007 gives a succinct summary of the weaknesses in the figures.

Data collection challenges for Cafcass in family proceedings and wider are also briefly touched on in an earlier chapter.

The Family Justice Review

This comprehensive government-commissioned 228-page report was published in November 2011.[40] Guiding principles that are identified to provide a framework – within which the review's work is expected to be undertaken – are set out in the report's Appendix A. The first seven paragraphs of the executive summary state:

> 1. We published our interim report[41] in March. This is our final report, which reflects our conclusions following well over 600 responses to our consultation and input from meetings in many parts of the country. We have also had the benefit of the Justice Select Committee's report on the operation of the family courts, published in July.
>
> 2. This final report aims to be a free-standing document but does not analyse the issues facing the family justice system in the detail of the interim report.[42] It sets out our final recommendations for reform, highlighting where these have changed and where they have not. It also includes expanded sections on the involvement of children and on workforce development.
>
> *Why Change Is Needed*
>
> 3. The family justice system deals with the failure of families, of parenting and of relationships, often involving anger, violence, abuse, drugs and alcohol. The decisions taken by local authorities and courts have fundamental long-term consequences for children, parents and for society generally.
>
> 4. There was general agreement that the legal framework is robust. We should be proud of this and in particular the core principle that the welfare of the child should be the paramount consideration in all decisions affecting them.
>
> 5. But the family justice system also faces immense stresses and difficulties. Some apply only in public law or private law but others are more systemic. Respondents to the consultation shared our deep concern about the way the system currently operates, and there was widespread agreement about our diagnosis.

---

[40] Family Justice Review Final Report (publishing.service.gov.uk)

[41] https://assets.publishing.service.gov.uk/media/5a7c541ded915d338141e166/family-justice-review-interim-rep.pdf

[42] Ibid.

- Cases take far too long. With care and supervision cases now taking on average 56 weeks (61 weeks in care centres) the life chances of already damaged children are further undermined by the very system that is supposed to protect them. And in private law, an average of 32 weeks allows conflict to become further entrenched and temporary arrangements for the care of children to become the default.
- The cost both to the taxpayer and often the individual is high. Many respondents saw a need for increased spending. But we are not convinced that current resources are spent in the most efficient and effective way.
- Both children and adults are often confused about what is happening to them. The need to address this will rise with the likely increase in the number of people who represent themselves in private law cases.
- Organisational structures are complicated and overlapping, with no clear sense of leadership or accountability. No one looks at the performance of the system as a whole.
- Individuals and organisations across different parts of the family justice system too often do not trust each other.
- There is no set of shared objectives to bind agencies and professionals to a common goal and to support joint working and planning between them.
- Morale can be low and the status of those working in some parts of the system does not match the levels of skill and commitment.
- Information and IT are wholly inadequate to support effective management and processes.

The Family Justice System

6. These issues show a set of arrangements in a slow building crisis. Family justice does not operate as a coherent, managed system. In fact, in many ways, it is not a system at all. Our proposals aimed to address this and focus on:

- ensuring the voices of children and young people are heard, and that they understand the decisions that affect them;
- the creation of a dedicated, managed Family Justice Service;
- the need for improved judicial leadership and a change in judicial culture;
- improvements to case management;
- ensuring the way in which the courts are organised is streamlined and more effective; and
- ensuring there is a competent and capable workforce, through effective workforce development.

7. Our proposals are designed to work in tandem with the reforms to child protection practice recommended by Professor Eileen Munro and with the work of the Social Work Reform Board.

Government Response to the Family Justice Review

This report was published in February 2012[43] and gives a detailed response to each of the Family Justice Review's recommendations. Its joint ministerial foreword is signed off by The Right Honourable Ken Clarke, Secretary of State for Justice, and The Right Honourable Michael Gove, Secretary of State for Education.

Its optimistic tone includes:

> This formal response is the start of the new phase of this work. It marks the beginning of a culture change, one that is particularly critical for faster resolution of care cases. We do not propose all the immediate answers here. The changes we pursue will not happen overnight – we must be clear about that from the start to maintain momentum. Our commitment will be strong and sustained. A lot of what is outlined here is ambitious – but we know that both those who work in the current system, and those who are affected by it, are crying out for a vision to unite behind. We look forward to seeing the first changes take effect, and to a new system of family justice taking root.

Explaining the structure of the government's response, the report goes on to state:

> 1. This response sets out our vision for how the Government, working with key partners, will reform the family justice system, improving it for the children and families who come into contact with it. Our ambitions are radical and will take time to implement, but the will and the appetite to make a difference is undeniable.
> 2. We have grouped our responses to the Family Justice Review Panel's recommendations according to the themes in the main body of their report. We begin with a child-centred system, as this is the central principle on which all the other reforms are based. We then consider the changes we will make to public and private law, and finally, we discuss how these changes play into a new system of family justice and what this means for more effective joint working between those professionals operating within it.
> 3. We are very pleased to be able to accept the overwhelming majority of the recommendations which the Panel made. Annex 1 sets out the response to each individual recommendation, our rationale for doing so, and the detailed changes we will make.

[43] https://assets.publishing.service.gov.uk/government/uploads/system/uploads/attachment_data/file/177097/CM-8273.pdf

> 4. This work requires drive and we intend to work at pace. In some areas we need to do more preparatory work before we can make sizeable changes, and we will engage families, those working on the ground and our partners as we do this, to make sure those changes are done in the right way but still at the earliest opportunity. A high-level timetable of when key changes will be made is in section J. We look forward to working closely with a wide-range of partners as early as possible in the process as we take forward the more detailed work.

Assessing the extent to which the above have been achieved since 2012 lies beyond the scope of this book, although the section below – the Children and Families Act 2014 – was a significant legislative step.

The Children and Families Act

On 13 March 2014, the Children and Families Act 2014 received royal assent, heralding reforms of the family justice system as part of the relaunch of the family court system. Family Justice and Civil Liberties Minister Simon Hughes' comments include:[44]

- 'We are making sure the welfare of children is at the heart of the family justice system.'
- 'We want to keep families away from the negative effects that going to court can have and to use alternative solutions when they are suitable. This is why we have changed the law to make sure that separating couples always consider mediation as an alternative to a courtroom battle.'
- 'When cases go to court we want them to happen in the least damaging way. So we are improving processes, reducing excessive delays, and we have also changed the law so that care cases must be completed within 26 weeks.'
- The new family court will make a number of changes behind the scenes which will make it operate more efficiently for court users.'

The explanatory notes[45] accompanying the Act provide a helpful overview. They summarise the main changes in both private and public law proceedings:

---

[44] https://www.gov.uk/government/news/major-changes-in-family-courts

[45] Children and Families Act 2014 - Explanatory Notes (legislation.gov.uk)

10. Part 2 makes changes to improve the operation of the family justice system, as recommended by the independent Family Justice Review and accepted by the Government in its response published on 6 February 2012. The Family Justice Review, chaired by David Norgrove, was set up by the Government in 2010 to look at the family justice system and make recommendations as to how the system could be changed for the benefit of children and families. An Interim Report was published in March 2011 and the Family Justice Review Final Report was published in November 2011.

11. In respect of private family law (by which is meant the law about resolving disputes between family members, as distinct from public family law, about intervention by public authorities), the Act includes provisions to:

- Require a potential applicant to attend a family mediation, information and assessment meeting to find out about and consider mediation before being able to apply for certain types of court order;
- Send a clear signal to separated parents that courts will take account of the principle that both should continue to be involved in their children's lives where that is safe and consistent with the child's welfare, which remains the court's paramount consideration;
- Introduce a 'child arrangements order', replacing residence and contact orders;
- Make changes so that when a child arrangements order is breached, the court can direct the parties to undertake activities designed to help them understand the importance of complying with the order and making it work;
- Streamline court processes in proceedings for a decree of divorce, nullity of marriage, or judicial separation (or, in relation to a civil partnership, for a dissolution, nullity or separation order) by removing the requirement for the court to consider whether it should exercise any of its powers under the Children Act 1989. Arrangements for children can be decided at any time through separate proceedings under the Children Act 1989.

12. In respect of public family law, the Act includes provisions to:

- Introduce a maximum 26-week time limit for completing care and supervision proceedings with the possibility of extending the time limit in a particular case for up to eight weeks at a time, should that be necessary to resolve the proceedings justly;
- Ensure that the timetable for the case is child focused and decisions about it are made with explicit reference to the child's welfare;

- Make it explicit that, when the court considers a care plan, it should focus on those issues essential to deciding whether to make a care order; and
- Remove the eight-week time limit on the duration of initial interim care orders and interim supervision orders, and the four-week time limit on subsequent orders, and allow the court to make interim orders for the length of time it sees fit, although not extending beyond the date when the relevant care or supervision order proceedings are disposed of.

Care Cases – the Looming Crisis

In his *View from the President's Chambers,* Sir James Mumby[46] presented a powerful overview of the position as of 2017:[47]

> In the meantime – today – we face a clear and imminent crisis. What steps can be taken now? The first thing is to do everything we properly can without sacrificing what is fundamental or prejudicing standards to improve the way in which we handle care cases:
>
> - Too many documents are still too long. Following the consultation earlier this year I will be amending … the Bundles Practice Direction, to impose page limits for certain categories of documents.
> - Local authority threshold statements need to be shorter, more focused …
> - Every effort must be made to ensure the effectiveness of the Case Management Hearing so as to avoid or at least minimise the need for further directions hearings.
> - More stringent scrutiny needs to be applied when applications for experts are being considered.
> - Every effort must be made to ensure the effectiveness of the IRH, so that the final hearing, if still required, focuses on what is really, and appropriately, in issue.
>
> The other thing is to continue to look for new, innovative and better ways of handling these cases, for example, by piloting and then rolling out the settlement conferences which I described in my last View. This is going to be uncomfortable and difficult for all of us. I have said before but I repeat, because the point is so important, that I will never countenance any departure from the fundamentals:
>
> - Care cases, with their potential for lifelong separation between children and their parents, are of unique gravity and importance.
> - It is for the local authority to establish its case.
> - Common-law principles of fairness and justice demand, as do Articles 6 and 8 of the Convention, a process in which both the parents and

[46] President of the Family Division 2013–2018.

[47] https://www.judiciary.uk/wp-content/uploads/2014/08/pfd-view-15-care-cases-looming-crisis.pdf

the child can fully participate with the assistance of representation by skilled and experienced lawyers.

- The tandem model is fundamental to a fair and just care system. Only the tandem model can ensure that the child's interests, wishes and feelings are correctly identified and properly represented. Without the tandem model the potential for injustice is much increased.

> I would therefore be strongly opposed to any watering down of this vital component of care proceedings. On the fundamentals there can be and will be neither compromise nor retreat. But this does not mean that there is no scope for improving, streamlining and speeding up our processes. We can, and we must, if the system is not to buckle under the pressure of ever-increasing caseloads. I have left until last the single-most important thing that can and must be done, urgently and with unremitting vigour, to manage the crisis.

The same view also lists suggestions where detailed research and analysis is urgently required in relation to judicial deployment in care cases and comments:

> One thing has emerged from such investigations as have so far taken place: there are many factors at play and none has a preponderating impact. The drivers are complex, with multiple drivers that have moderate or small impact creating a cumulative impact, rather than a small number of key drivers with high impact. Further research is desperately needed if we are to have any chance of coming up with accurate predictions for the future ... though whether the data exists is likely to be problematic in some instances.

More Recent Reflections

Discussing the voice of the child in family justice in 2018, Mervyn Murch also points out[48] that a major feature of modern family justice has been the increasing recognition being given to the voice of the child, particularly in the public law field. But he suggests this is less so in practice in private law because of economic constraints, although he comments that it may not just be the current economic pressure that restricts the opportunities to take account of children's views when their parents divorce or separate. Murch raises a more fundamental issue to be considered, that with our culture there is a strong tendency to socially construct the process of family breakdown in purely adult terms.

Supporting children when parents separate, Chapter 4, Murch, M., Policy Press, 2018

Further Reports

The handling of private law disputes especially with regard to arrangements for children, have been the subject of many research reports, policy developments, proposals and related initiatives, both before and since Cafcass was established. Which issues should best be handled only within the court's jurisdiction and what might be better dealt with pre-court through a range of differently titled mediation services has a long history that largely falls outside this book's aims.

However, ongoing private law disputes, usually about arrangements for contact, continue to get adverse media coverage, sometimes backed by research. *The Guardian's* 20 July 2020 article is but one example[49] and covers a report published by the Ministry of Justice in June 2020.[50] Two paragraphs of the report's executive summary state:

> 6. The legal framework set out in the Children Act 1989 requires the court to give paramount consideration to the welfare of the child. Despite this, the evidence submitted to the panel demonstrates continuing concerns around how the family court system recognises and responds to allegations of, and proven harm to, children and victim parents in private law children proceedings.
>
> 7. Whilst the panel has identified some good practice and widespread good intentions from those working under increasing pressure within the family justice system, it has also unveiled deep-seated and systematic issues that were found to affect how risk to both children and adults is identified and managed.

The report also highlights several specific issues, none of which will come as a surprise to many informed readers:

> 8. ... The panel found these issues were underpinned by the following key themes in the evidence that was reviewed:
>
> - Resource constraints; resources available have been inadequate to keep up with increasing demand in private law children proceedings, and more parties are coming to court unrepresented.
> - The pro-contact culture; respondents felt that courts placed undue priority on ensuring contact with the non-resident parent, which resulted in systemic minimisation of allegations of domestic abuse.

---

[49] https://www.theguardian.com/society/2020/jul/28/twisted-priorities-mean-cafcass-has-failed-to-protect-children-from-abusive-parents

[50] https://assets.publishing.service.gov.uk/government/uploads/system/uploads/attachment_data/file/895173/assessing-risk-harm-children-parents-pl-childrens-cases-report_.pdf

- Working in silos; submissions highlighted differences in approaches and culture between criminal justice, child protection (public law) and private law children proceedings, and lack of communication and coordination between family courts and other courts and agencies working with families, which led to contradictory decisions and confusion.
- An adversarial system; with parents placed in opposition on what is often not a level playing field in cases involving domestic abuse, child sexual abuse and self-representation, with little or no involvement of the child.

The report also makes a number of recommendations.

Transparency

On 29 October 2021, President of the Family Division, Sir Andrew McFarlane, made the following announcement:[51]

> The present system in the Family Court whereby a journalist may attend any hearing but may not always report what they observe, is not sustainable. I have reached the conclusion that there needs to be a major shift in culture and process to increase the transparency in a number of respects. The conclusions that I have reached, following an extensive review, are published today. The review has focused upon the dual goals of enhancing public confidence in the Family Justice system, whilst at the same time maintaining the anonymity of those families and children who turn to it for protection. These twin principles of confidence and confidentiality are not, in my view, mutually exclusive, and it is possible to achieve both goals.
>
> In addition to a range of ancillary proposals, my main conclusion is that the time has come for accredited media representatives to be able, not only to attend hearings, but to report publicly on what they see and hear. Any reporting must, however, be subject to very clear rules to maintain the anonymity of children and families, and to keep confidential intimate details of their private lives.
>
> I now intend to lead the process of implementing these changes, which will involve a number of initiatives. Any change in the court process will require the approval of the Family Procedure Rules Committee and Ministry of Justice ministers. Insofar as there is a need to amend statute law, this is, of course, a matter entirely for Parliament and not the judiciary.

Background papers were published at the same time.[52] The programme has been gradually extended in subsequent stages.

---

[51] https://www.judiciary.uk/guidance-and-resources/transparency-in-the-family-courts-report-3/

[52] https://www.judiciary.uk/wp-content/uploads/2021/10/Confidence-and-Confidentiality-Transparency-in-the-Family-Courts-final.pdf

Further Consultation

Still further consultation continues, for example as announced by the Ministry of Justice in March 2023.[53] The foreword by the deputy prime minister and Justice Secretary includes comment on supporting earlier resolution of private family law arrangements:

> With an impressive 69 percent success rate, the scheme has made it possible for over 13,500 families to enlist the help of mediators and reach full or partial agreements, without the need to go through a potentially long and adversarial court process ... We are determined to build on that success – to make sure that, where it is safe and appropriate to do so, parties in private family law disputes make reasonable attempts to mediate and reach solutions before applying to the courts as a last resort. And we want to empower judges to hold accountable those who do not engage seriously with mediation, and who draw proceedings out unnecessarily by refusing to reach reasonable settlements.

Another Report

And a further example is a later 2023 report[54] that states that the government is ignoring millions of children caught up in divorce and separation, it could make savings if the system is reformed, and that children's rights are being ignored when couples separate or divorce.

Judith Timms OBE, lead author of the report and who has been referred to several times above in earlier chapters, says:

> The shocking stand-out finding from all the consultees was that this very large cohort of children are invisible in terms of public policy and service provision. There are large parts of the system that have no recognition of the vulnerability of children when parents separate and they have no one to speak up for them ... Given divorce is now easier since the introduction of no-fault divorce last year and given it is a common occurrence, we must not leave children's interests behind. The courts system is by its nature adversarial and sets an unhelpful context of there being sides, leaving children vulnerable in the middle.

[53] https://consult.justice.gov.uk/digital-communications/private-family-law-consultation/

[54] A-Childs-Right-to-Matter.pdf (familysolutionsgroup.co.uk)

Memorial Lecture

And finally in this chapter, delivering The Nicholas Wall Memorial Lecture in May 2023, Lord Justice Peter Jackson titled his address 'Is Family Law Law?',[55] and he comments:

> A further aspect of family law is that it is usually more concerned with prediction than other branches of law ... the family court may be asking whether a parent injured a child, but for it that is not the ultimate question. It has to go on and look to the future and ask itself what sort of a person this parent is. If they did it before, will they do it again? This involves an effort to understand what the person is really like and then to work out what the child really needs. The decision may have lifelong consequences, and the court must take the initiative in trying to get it right. That responsibility does not generally exist in civil and criminal proceedings.

And he also points out:

> One consequence of the welfare objective is that the most deserving litigant is not always successful. Privileging the child's welfare may lead to uncomfortable results. In care cases, the parents may have had truly terrible childhoods themselves, and it is particularly disturbing that mothers who are the victims of severe domestic abuse may lose their children if they cannot escape the cycle of their own oppression. If they are trapped in it, the welfare principle is society's painful way of breaking the cycle for the good of the child in a way that can be extremely unfair to the mother. This is not soft law. In times past, the idea seemed to be abroad, including at the Judicial Appointments Commission, that sensitivity was the distinctive requirement for a family judge. Now, there is a general recognition that sensitivity, necessary as it is, won't get you far without toughness.

---

[55] https://www.judiciary.uk/the-nicholas-wall-memorial-lecture-given-by-lord-justice-peter-jackson-is-amily-law-law/#related_content

10

Inspectorates

This chapter explores some historical inspectorate issues and also discusses changes across the wider inspectorate landscape alongside comments from the chief inspector's[1] annual report and in other inspection reports on Cafcass.

The Probation Inspectorate

The HM Inspectorate of Probation was established in 1937.[2] Although inspections of family court welfare were undertaken by it in 1990 and 1997,[3] it is doubtful that any of its later recommendations as addressed to probation committees, chief probation officers, the president of the Family Division and the Home Office were implemented before the idea of unifying the family court welfare services gathered momentum in 1998.

The Social Work Service

The 1968 committee report, chaired by Frederic Seebohm, is a landmark publication.[4] In its discussion about the relationship between central and local government in running the personal social services, the committee states:[5]

> In our view, central government has three essential functions to perform in relation to the local government services ...
> (i) It must in planning for the future decide what the aims of the service are, and make sure that local authorities understand those decisions.
> (ii) It must set and ensure minimum levels of service over the country as a whole.
> (iii) It must collect and disseminate relevant and useful information about the services and the needs they ought to be trying to meet.

---

[1] The post-holder's full title is 'Her Majesty's Chief Inspector of Education, Children's Services and Skills' (Education and Inspections Act 2006 s 113)

[2] https://www.justiceinspectorates.gov.uk/hmiprobation/wp-content/uploads/sites/5/2023/10/The-history-of-HMI-Probation.pdf

[3] HM Inspectorate of Probation - *Family Court Welfare Work: Report of a Thematic Inspection,* London: Home Office (1997)

[4] Report of The Committee on Local Authority and Allied Personal Social Services, Cmnd 3703, HMSO, 1968

[5] Ibid. paragraph 646

From these three principles, the committee draws three conclusions, the first being about funding; the second about allowing local authority discretion and the third the need for an inspectorate.[6] Of the last, they say:

> In order to carry out its functions effectively, the central government department concerned must have a strong, accessible and well-respected inspectorate to advise local authorities, to promote the achievement of aims and the maintenance of standards, and to act as two-way channels for information and consultation between central and local government.

And in words that may help explain some of the inspectorate approaches described later in this chapter, as well as earlier in this book, the committee writes:[7]

> It does not necessarily follow that the new inspectorate would adopt the methods of any one of the present government departments concerned. We see the role of the inspectorate as not so much regulatory as promotional, educational and consultative ... The emphasis on this kind of work will certainly require an expansion in the central government inspectorate and the recruitment of officers of high quality.

The Social Services Inspectorate

The Social Services Inspectorate (SSI) was established in 1985. I was appointed to it shortly afterwards. Background details about the inspectorate were laid out in a written reply given by the then Secretary of State for Social Services, Mr. Kenneth Clarke, and included:[8]

> In April 1983 ... chairmen of all social services committees [were sent] a consultative document proposing development of our Department's social work service—which already exercises inspectorial functions—explicitly into an inspectorate for the local authority social services ... the Government have now reached agreement in principle with the local authority associations on the way forward ... The inspectorate will assist local authorities to obtain value for money through the efficient and economic use of available resources. Its aim will be to help to secure the most effective use of professional and other resources, normally by identifying good practice and spreading knowledge about it.
>
> Inspections will be of 3 main types:

Ibid. paragraph 647

Ibid. paragraph 649

Social Service Inspectorate (Hansard, 25 February 1985) (parliament.uk)

(a) initiated by Ministers and the Department in exercise of the Secretary of State's formal powers of inspection;
(b) undertaken outside formal powers, related to issues of general concern and covering a number of local authorities, by agreement with the authorities concerned and in accordance with a programme agreed by the local authority associations; and
(c) undertaken outside formal powers, but at the request of, or in agreement with, an individual local authority and in relation to specific services or activities of that authority.

Reports written as a result of formal inspections will be made in the first instance to the Secretary of State, but all other reports will be made concurrently to the authorities concerned for their social services committees to see. Reports will normally be documents of public access. Formally, the existing statutory powers of inspection (which are considered sufficient for the purposes of the new Inspectorate) are vested in the Secretary of State, and he will be the Minister responsible for the Inspectorate's management and actions.

... the programme of work of the Inspectorate outside formal powers will be a joint concern of central and local government. This will be reflected in a Steering Group of representatives of the Department and the local authority associations, with the following terms of reference:

To consider the proposals of the Social Services Inspectorate for inspections of local authority personal social services (other than those to be made under statutory powers, or in relation to specific services or activities of an individual authority at the request of or in agreement with that authority); to agree annually a programme of such inspections; and to review from time to time the scope for future work of the Inspectorate.

The staff of the Social Services inspectorate will consist of members of the existing Social Work Service, supplemented by staff from relevant disciplines on attachment from local authorities and other organisations, including experts in appropriate branches of management and in performance measurement. The Inspectorate will aim to complement, not compete with, the work of the Audit Commission and will continue existing collaboration with Her Majesty's Inspectorate of Schools, the Probation Inspectorate and the Health Advisory Service. The new inspectorate will come into operation on 1 April 1985 ...

Sir William Utting was appointed as its first chief inspector. Thirty-nin years later, he shared the following recollection with me:

Big decisions in government may be made overnight. Small ones can take longer. Converting a professional advisory service into an inspectorate cut across the values of other professions and was at odds with a policy of 'getting off the backs of local government'. The latter feared a possible instrument for cost-cutting, while the Treasury warned of writing blank cheques for what it regarded as profligate authorities. Support came from a parliamentary committee, senior civil servants and – crucially – the Minister for Health, Kenneth Clarke. The local authorities were engaged as partners; and inspectorial methods accepted as contributing to the government's policy of 'Value for Money'. The process spanned nine years of intermittent work.

SSI London Region

On arrival at the Social Services Inspectorate London Region in 1985 and over the next few years, a number of responsibilities allocated to me fall outside the main scope of this chapter. They include:

- inspection prior to Secretary of State approval of voluntary children's homes and secure accommodation units;
- inspection of local authority child protection services;
- establishing and maintaining a good level of mutual rapport with three London directors of social services in order to effect fast two-way communications on urgent matters. Where necessary, the SSD directors were alerted to important pending government announcements and ministers were briefed by the SSI if a serious incident had occurred within the local authority SSD remit, around which publicity, possibly unfavourable, might be expected or had already occurred

Throughout this period, the London region was led by an inspirational and hardworking assistant chief inspector in David Lambert. He was also much respected by London directors of social services. On his retirement, he was awarded the CBE and he hosted an impressive party at his Suffolk home for colleagues, friends and family. We remained in contact until shortly before his death in October 2010. An obituary by a former colleague and London director of social services was published in The Guardian later that year.[9]

Youth Treatment Centres

Leading the multi-inspectorate inspections in 1987 of the DHSS's (later the DH's) two youth treatment centres (YTCs) at Glenthorne, sited in

https://www.theguardian.com/society/2010/dec/01/david-lambert-obituary

Erdington, Birmingham, and St Charles, located at Brentwood, Essex, were the most complex and challenging inspections I ever undertook. Among the many serious problems revealed were:

- weak leadership and management at both centres and by the responsible government department (DHSS)
- that the former YTC was run on ill-applied behaviour modification lines; the latter on damaging psychotherapeutic principles
- high levels of abuse of children's human rights and degrading treatment of them in contravention of the European Convention Human Rights

The large inspectorate team was assembled from several SSI regions and Ofsted HMI, as well as with input from the DHSS, covering the fields of psychiatry, psychology, architects, nursing and dieticians. I recall:

YTC staff came from three backgrounds – health, residential care and education. All had kept their original terms and conditions, which meant huge pay disparities for similar work. The first sign of open defiance was when staff at a meeting at one of the YTCs refused to tell the HMI their names.

I also recall:

During one evening inspectorate debriefing meeting, in a moment of intuition I crossed to the conference room door and opened it suddenly. Squatting outside trying to listen to our meeting was the head of one of YTC's units.

Glenthorne

Glenthorne was a purpose-built residential treatment centre for young people which opened in 1978. It could accommodate, at the time of its opening, 62 children aged between 12 and 19. The children coming into Glenthorne had each been sent there from the courts.[10] The centre was not run by Birmingham City Council but by the Department of Health as a national resource. By 1998 the number of beds in the centre had been reduced to 30. It was closed in July 2002.

St Charles

St Charles opened in 1971. On 29 June 1995 Health Minister, John Bowi announced the intention to close the St Charles youth treatment centre:

[10] Under powers derived from the Children and Young Person Act 1933, section 53

> I am no longer satisfied that the centre can continue in the future to provide properly for the best interests of the young people accommodated there or for those of the staff or for the security of the local community. The centre was designed and built in the 1960s and the buildings no longer meet accepted standards. There have also been problems of management and control which have proved difficult to resolve. In consequence, the centre has been operating far below its nominal capacity and currently accommodates only 6 young people.

Reasons for the eventual closure of both centres were presented by the department's senior management and ministers as being on economic grounds, whereas in the inspectorate's view, the most pressing concerns were those of child welfare and a serious lack of protection for them from physical, sexual and emotional harm, mainly inflicted by staff.

Adoption Act 1976

Pre-approval inspections of London-based voluntary adoption societies were required as part of the statutory arrangements. The organisations operated under the provisions laid down in section 3 of the Adoption Act 1976[11] and its supporting regulations. While most functioned to commendable professional standards, there was a small minority that struggled to do so and needed a great deal of support from the SSI to adapt to the new legal requirements of the Adoption Agencies Regulations 1983.[12]

Writing in 2001, I noted:

> One particular complaint in 1996 came directly to the Prime Minister's Office from a person who had accepted the post of director of a highly regarded voluntary adoption agency but had withdrawn when she discovered that it and a local authority had worked closely to effect a placement of a 15-year-old Down's syndrome girl in circumstances of which she strongly disapproved. I was instructed to investigate by No. 10.
>
> After several interviews with the adoption agency and the local authority, I confirmed that everything had been done with great care and entirely within the requirements of the regulations. The child had been looked after by the local authority for some years, but previous attempts to secure an adoptive placement for her had not been successful. New prospective adopters had been found; both were quite young qualified nurses with the disabled. Both were male. I submitted my report to No. 10 and heard nothing more. Later, the High Court granted the adoption order.

1 Adoption Act 1976 (legislation.gov.uk)

2 https://www.legislation.gov.uk/uksi/1983/1964/made

Around this time, one large organisation with a high reputation for it work with families wanted to extend its activities and become a established adoption agency. I recall:

> Meeting one of the organisation's managers at my office and going through all the legal requirements before inviting her to contact me again when they were ready for me to undertake a formal inspection. Later, after several days of intensive scrutiny and accompanied by numerous cups of tea and tempting cakes, my report recommending approval was dispatched, and shortly after, the Secretary of State gave her consent.

However, no such inspection or approval was required when it came t local authorities, all of whom had to provide an adoption service unde the 1976 Adoption Act. I sought and obtained agreement that the Socia Services Inspectorate should undertake some pilot inspections of loca authority adoption services. I enlisted the help of three experienced fiel practitioners as temporary co-inspectors. Having next designed th methodology, the three inspections were undertaken in London i 1990/1991. They proved revealing – and mainly highly critical. By th mid-1990s such adoption inspections were incorporated routinely into th SSI's work programme, and these were later passed on to successc Inspectorates covering local authority children's services.

Inspection of the Galro Service

As noted in an earlier chapter, the first inspection of the Galro service i England by the Social Services Inspectorate was undertaken in 1989/199(just before the Children Act 1989 came into force. It was quite influentia on the department's thinking about the 1991 Galro panel regulations an the need to reduce the number of people on panels – then about 5,000 to a more sensible figure that better reflected the amount of availabl work. As too many only undertook one or two cases a year, a mor concentrated workforce of about 1,500 was considered necessary. Progres towards this aim was partly achieved by 2001, when there were about 24 employed guardians and 750 self- employed across England and Wale dealing with about 13,000 care-related and adoption cases per year.[13]

Two further inspections of Galro panels were undertaken by the Socia Services Inspectorate[14] in 1993 and in 1994/95. Both had the sam

---

[13] A report on the findings and key issues arising from and inspection of three panels. *'What does it mean for us?'*, SSI (1993)

[14] A report on the findings and key issues arising from and inspection of four panels, 1994/5, SSI, 199

bjectives – namely, to contribute to the Department of Health's overall ssessment of the impact of the Children Act 1989; to report on the quality f guardian work in care-related proceedings; and to make ecommendations to assist panels in maintaining and improving the ervice. Both inspections used the National Standards for the Galro ervice, which were being developed by the Department of Health in close onsultation with local Galro services.[15] These were discussed in Chapter 2.

Among the key inspectorate findings reported in 1993 was a generally igh quality of services being offered to children, their families and carers, vith most guardians able to demonstrate their impartiality in their rofessional practice. However, there was still a need for panel ommittees, managers, guardians and administering local authorities to esolve existing confusion about the differing concepts of professional ndependence and accountability. There was a generally held view that ne government guidance was insufficiently detailed in this key area.

hildren Act Studies Undertaken by the Department of Iealth

ecause much commissioned research might take three or four years to e finalised and published, something else was needed within a shorter mescale to investigate problems associated with implementing the Act. Vith Rupert Hughes' support, we proposed short Children Act studies nat would be rather like confidential enquiries, getting everyone in an nterdisciplinary network to talk about issues without identifying in the ublished report their names or the agencies for which they worked. They ould point the way for more thorough research or for guidance. I led on everal SSI studies the main messages of which are summarised in the 001 messages from research referred to earlier in Chapter 2. Two of the udies are discussed below.

lanning Long-term Placement Study

n March 1993 five local authorities and a national voluntary child care rganisation met the Social Services Inspectorate (SSI) to express concern bout the way the Children Act 1989 was operating. Their focus was round children being looked after by local authorities and the way in vhich long-term planning issues for these children were being

National Standards for the Guardian ad Litem and Reporting Officer Service, Department of Health nd Welsh Office (1995)

approached by both social workers and courts. It was further considered that social workers were experiencing confusion about permanency and contact. Instances were cited where social workers had included proposals for contact in court reports even where they did not feel it was in the child's interests. This had been done because of advice from their own legal departments that courts would not accept a plan that did not include contact.

The study[16] I wrote with colleagues was commissioned as a partial response to such concerns and to test out in a number of local authorities the above views. The preface to the report, also written by me, said:

> Child care theory and practice is full of tensions. The concerns about children who drifted in care led to more vigorous polices intended to promote the concept of permanence. The difficulty remains that of reaching sound judgements – which course is likely to achieve the best results for the child. Determining the welfare of the child is not a straightforward matter. The next few weeks or months may be crucial – but so too are the years ahead – all the years of childhood. Near the centre of concern must be the quality of decision-making and the quality of life which the child actually experiences. Achieving permanence cannot be an end in itself. A permanent placement is not necessarily a happy one for the child.

Local authorities were asked to produce examples of such difficulties. The study sought to evaluate from a retrospective viewpoint that under the Children Act 'things are worse'. The study tried to establish the elements of policy, practice, personnel, legal powers and other statutory duties that contribute to the key decisions about long-term placements.
The report emphasises:

> This study is not an inspection and it does not evaluate or explore the quality of casework decisions or comment on the legality of local authority actions. Its focus is to gather information and views in support of their assertions that certain types of child care planning are more difficult now than under previous legislation.
>
> No details are included in the report which might identify children, local authority staff or the participating authorities. The four authorities were a South of England County Council; a Midlands Council; a Northern Metropolitan Council; and a London Borough.

[16] The Children Act 1989, Planning Long term Placements Study, Department of Health 1994

The 66 children in the study were born between 1977 and 1993, broadly balanced between boys and girls and included a range of ethnic and religious backgrounds. The report details the methodologies used during the study. Towards the end of the study, a wider national consultation meeting was held involving local authorities and voluntary organisations, which afforded further opportunity to discuss long-term planning issues for children under the Children Act in the context of the study.

The study's findings did not confirm the widely held belief that under the Children Act it was more difficult to plan and achieve long-term placements for children. The report's concluding comments state:

> In a number of cases, planning itself was underdeveloped, and this was not a failure of the Act but of assessment processes and not coming to a clear enough view of the child's needs and how they should be met. In other cases – too many – there were concerns about court delay ... However, there was little evidence of local authorities making strenuous representations to their local courts to help ensure that timetables were kept to the minimum.

And my final comments add:

> Many of the cases were complex and difficult to manage. They would, it is suggested, present such difficulties in any legislative framework. There will always be a proportion of cases where the problems of the children and their families are complicated, cumulative and enduring. This is especially so when there are the interests of the other children in the family to consider. Changes of social worker, lack of specialist skills, local reorganisation and delays in implementing parts of the agreed plan will all have an impact on successfully achieving long-term placements. Although the study raises important concerns and questions about the effectiveness of local authority planning, assessment and case management, no major fault lines are revealed in the Act itself.

The Timetabling of Interim Care Orders Study

This 1994 study was commissioned by the Department of Health from external consultants.[17] It aimed 'to explore the reasons for the time taken to complete care proceedings in a number of cases selected on the basis of their length and to examine the causes of delay'. Its final chapter discusses a range of emerging issues. Prior to publication the Department of Health convened a meeting of local authority solicitors and social workers who had not been part of the study, together with guardian panel managers, researchers and DH and LCD personnel. It provided a useful

[17] The Children Act 1989: Timetabling of Interim Care Order Study, Plotnikoff, J., Woolfson, R., SSI, 1994

opportunity to compare the study findings with the experience of attendees, some whose views are also included in the study. Fifteen suggestions of 'good practice proposals' are included in the final chapter of the study.

The Magistrates' Courts Services Inspectorate

Kit Chivers, Chief Inspector MCSI, recalls:

> *I had never heard of the proposed Cafcass when the junior minister called me to her office and asked me how I felt about taking it on. I simply said 'Yes, of course, Minister', trusting that it would all work out.*

The Criminal Justice and Court Services Act 2000 sets out the duty of the Magistrates' Courts Service Inspectorate (MCSI) to inspect and report to the Lord Chancellor on Cafcass' performance. Powers of inspectors include a right of entry at reasonable times to Cafcass premises and also a right to access and take copies of any Cafcass records.[18]

Early in 2001 the MCSI drafted its three-year inspection strategy for Cafcass and obtained full LCD ministerial support for it. The MCSI then presented it to the Cafcass board on 15 April 2001. At that meeting inspectors explained that the first phase of inspections would start in June with a series of 'structured visits' and continue until December with visits to all Cafcass areas and headquarters. This would result in the production of a baseline report in March 2002.[19] This would be followed by a series of 'baseline inspections' from April 2002. Full inspections would begin from April 2003, and each area, including headquarters, could be expected to be inspected every three years.

This approach did not start with formal inspections. Instead, the 'structured visits' afforded the opportunity to test and develop appropriate inspection methodologies and build up the MCSI's inspection team. A second overview report, 'Setting a Course', covered the baseline inspections and was published in 2003.

Kit Chivers, Chief Inspector MCSI, also recalls:

> *Interviewing officers from the two separate traditions ... and reflecting on how disparate the cultures were and how difficult it would be to bring them together ... one barely had time for a single interview with a family, while the others were able to visit many times over a period of months and build up a relationship with the families. It was always going to be difficult to find*

[18] Criminal Justice and Court Services Act 2000, section 17 (1) and (2)

[19] Setting Up was published in March 2002.

> *a reasonable compromise ... I had admiration for both sets of professionals and for the judiciary ... and it was brought home to me how extraordinarily difficult those judgements are. The judges themselves said that taking a child away from its mother was harder than sentencing someone to life imprisonment.*

In its report on Cafcass' first few months, published in March 2002, the MCSI reported:

> Setting a culture and style for governance of any organisation is important. This process can be distorted if, through necessity or for other reasons, key people are temporarily acting out of role and there is, in consequence, a lack of clarity about respective responsibilities. There was evidence of some confusion around the respective functions of key organisational elements, including—the Board, its Chairman and its Sub-Committees or Working Groups;— the Chief Executive and the Senior Management Team;— the interfaces between CAFCASS as a Non Departmental Public Body and its sponsoring organisation, the LCD.

Disappointingly, save for a few exceptions, none of the MCSI and HMICA reports on inspections of Cafcass from 2002 to 2006 have survived online. When these inspectorates ceased to operate, their two websites were deleted by the responsible government department for reasons that remain unknown. This may pose a significant challenge for anyone researching this area of family law in future years.

Cafcass' Summary of Inspections

Covering both MCSI and HMICA inspections, Cafcass' annual report for 2004–05[20] states:

> During the reporting period, the HM Magistrates' Courts Service Inspectorate (MCSI) continued its programme of Phase Three inspections and undertook five post-inspection reviews and two joint thematic reviews. MCSI migrated into HM Inspectorate of Court Administration (HMICA) on 1 April 2005. Phase Three inspections covered the National Office, South West and Eastern regions, Recruitment and First Line Management.
>
> The Post Inspection Reviews completed during the year were CAFCASS Legal Services and the East Midlands, North East, South East and Yorkshire and Humberside regions. The reviews focused on the extent to which the implementation of 22 MCSI recommendations resulting from earlier baseline inspections had been implemented. Of the 22 recommendations, four

---

[20] https://www.gov.uk/government/publications/children-and-family-court-advisory-and-support-service-annual-report-and-accounts-2004-to-2005

(18.2%) had been implemented fully, 17 (77.3%) had been partially implemented, with further work being undertaken, and one recommendation had not been implemented.

The MCSI placed the overall performance regarding the implementation of their recommendations in the context of wider difficulties experienced by CAFCASS in previous years. The increased drive towards improvement in service delivery and, in particular, reducing delay were noted.

HMICA

In April 2005, Her Majesty's Courts Service (HMCS) was established under the Courts Act 2003, creating a unified court administration across England and Wales. At that date, Her Majesty's Court Service Inspectorate ceased to exist and became HM Inspectorate of Court Administration (HMICA). Its aims and responsibilities encompass those of the MCSI, but also extend them to the higher courts. As footnoted below, HMICA's duties to inspect court administration and Cafcass are set out in the Courts Act 2003.[21]

Thematic Review – Domestic Violence, Safety and Family Proceedings

HMICA's decision to undertake this thematic review in 2005 was influenced by inspections on domestic violence in criminal proceedings, including the Crown Prosecution Inspectorate and the Inspectorate of Constabulary joint thematic inspection Violence at Home (February 2004) and the HM Inspectorate of Probation report Reducing Domestic Violence (2004). HMICA's inspection was greatly assisted by a widely based advisory group that included HM Court Service and Cafcass.

The chief inspector's foreword to the report explains that:

> While it is the role of the criminal courts to deal with prosecutions involving domestic violence, family courts and CAFCASS frequently deal with similar allegations. Typically, these arise in disputed applications between parents,

[21] Section 59(1) (as amended) states, 'It is the duty of inspectors of court administration to:
(a) Inspect and report to the Lord Chancellor on the system that supports the carrying on of the business of the courts;
(b) Inspect and report to the Secretary of State on the performance of CAFCASS functions;
(c) Discharge any other particular functions which may be
(i) specified in connection with the courts listed in subsection (2) in a direction given by the Lord Chancellor, or
(ii) specified in connection with CAFCASS functions or related functions of any other person in a direction given by the Secretary of State.'
The Inspectorate is not empowered to inspect persons making judicial decisions or exercising any judicial discretion (Courts Act 2003, section 59(5))

> including those regarding the future arrangements for the children's residence and contact. This inspection looks at how family courts handle such issues in their administrative arrangements, particularly from the perspective of court users. We also report on CAFCASS' strategic management and its frontline practice when dealing with similar cases.

The foreword continues:

> This report finds an inherent danger arising from the current policy emphasis on seeking agreements between parents in ever larger numbers of disputed family proceedings. We conclude that ensuring the safety of both children and adults receives insufficient consideration – this was a strong and consistent message from the women survivors of domestic violence who we consulted. We consider that arrangements for assessing the risks associated with allegations of domestic violence need markedly strengthening. I am pleased to report examples of good practice in both Services. But the overall picture is less satisfactory. Both HMCS and CAFCASS need significantly to improve safety within their service delivery and the report's eleven recommendations are designed to assist that process.

And the foreword ends:

> We also need to recognise how emotionally wearing it is for a wide range of professionals who have to deal with domestic violence on a near daily basis. As this inspection shows, there is a risk that individuals within agencies sometimes find it easier to down-play or even ignore signs of domestic violence. Its serious and corrosive effects on both survivors and children require HMCS and CAFCASS to implement robust strategies to guide staff in how to handle cases where domestic violence is alleged, or is proven to be an issue, in the context of family proceedings. These are essential steps towards achieving improved sensitivity and effectiveness in service delivery for some of society's most vulnerable people.

Inspection of Private Law Practice

This HMICA inspection of Cafcass was undertaken between October 2005 and March 2006. Importantly, it broke entirely new ground by including for the first time in its methodology direct observation of Cafcass practitioners' front-line work[22] when interviewing parents and children.

The chief inspector's foreword to the report said:

> During the last year, issues concerning the family justice system have had a high public and political profile. That is likely to continue. When courts dealing with family proceedings consider contested applications, they turn

https://www.voiceofthechild.org.uk/wp-content/uploads/2017/10/Private-law-HMICA-report.pdf August 2006)

to CAFCASS for detailed social work advice to aid their decision-making. This occurs most frequently about contact and residence. CAFCASS 'front-line' practitioners undertake case planning, interviews and assessments, and prepare reports to court based on those assessments. It is demanding, difficult and skilled social work.

Most of what happens in CAFCASS interviews is not seen by others. With the agreement of families, Inspectors observed interviews undertaken by CAFCASS staff from the start to the end of the case. Direct observation is a powerful tool and provided telling evidence for Inspectors. In bringing this information together, HMICA has been able to evaluate the quality of CAFCASS front-line practice in its private law work. I am pleased that HMICA's report identifies examples of good practice.

But I am also concerned that too many of our findings echo key messages from our previous reports. In particular:

- There is still a strong culture of localised custom and practice.
- CAFCASS' new quality assurance mechanisms, introduced in 2005, have not yet made a real impact on front-line practice.
- Scarce resources are being wasted when reports are prepared, even though there are no significant child welfare issues.
- Assessments, including those focused on the risk of domestic violence, are weak.

I conclude that CAFCASS urgently needs to strengthen the effectiveness of its efforts to drive both change and higher standards of front-line practice. Our recommendations aim to help CAFCASS achieve tangible improvements in the quality and consistency of its services to children and families.

Inspection of Public Law Practice

This HMICA inspection of Cafcass was undertaken between January and March 2007 and concerned front-line practice in care proceedings. The chief inspector's foreword said:

> The decisions that the family courts reach in such cases are serious and far-reaching – both for the child and the child's wider family. For the State to intervene so decisively into family life, the courts must be satisfied that the legal criteria are met, that an order is necessary and that the local authority's care plan will meet the child's immediate and long-term needs to the greatest extent practicable.

Commenting on the practice of children's guardians, the foreword continued:

> Much of their work is good enough, but some is not. There are practice weaknesses that need to be addressed urgently in order to ensure that:

- the parents' capacity to parent their child is assessed in a robust, fair and transparent manner;
- similar standards apply when children's guardians advise on contact between a looked-after child and a parent;
- the guardian's scrutiny of the local authority care plan is credible, and grounded in a thorough, systematic, Cafcass-wide, approved approach.

Five recommendations are made that aim to help Cafcass bring about important improvement.

Practitioner Accountability

From 1984 onwards, court rules laid out both mandatory duties and permissive discretionary powers for guardians appointed in care-related proceedings – and where necessary for courts to terminate a guardian's appointment. No other form of social work was so tightly prescribed. But there was often confusion within the service, which continued for some years into Cafcass, about whether the primary accountability of the appointed guardian was to the court or to the child or to the employing authority. This led to further questions about how discretion and independent professional judgement were exercised by individual practitioners.

As part of the inspection of public law practice, HMICA sent out a questionnaire to children's guardians in four Cafcass regions, which produced 194 responses. They were asked to whom they saw themselves accountable for various tasks. Responses showed a high proportion of children's guardians who see themselves as having a shared accountability between the courts and Cafcass.

HMICA summarised these views in its report as:

Shared responsibility

- nearly half (48%) saw accountability for how they plan and carry out their investigations in a case as shared between the courts and Cafcass
- similarly, two thirds (68%) for quality standards in the report
- slightly less (61%) for the time taken in the case
- half (54%) for the recommendation.

Accountability to the Court

- one in seven (16%) of children's guardians saw their accountability as mainly to the court for how they plan and carry out their investigation in a case
- nearly a third (29%) saw their accountability for their recommendation as lying with the court

- a number made an explicit reference to their role as 'Officers of the Court'.

HMICA's report continues:

> The confusion about who is accountable to whom and about what is particularly unhelpful. Until that is clarified, such confusion will pose ongoing problems for Cafcass' management of public law proceedings. Cafcass senior management may well need to work closely with government departments and the family judiciary to resolve these issues. For that reason, having drawn attention to the importance of the matter, HMICA does not consider that it would be helpful to make this the subject of a formal recommendation.

Cafcass set up an accountability review headed by an experienced regional manager, which helped bring a degree of clarity and consistency of approach across the service.

Inspection in Wales

The transfer of Cafcass responsibilities to the Welsh Assembly was first suggested in 2003 as a result of the transfer of sponsorship responsibilities for Cafcass from the Department of Constitutional Affairs (DCA) to the Department for Education and Skills (DfES). The transfer team was established in May 2004. There was a period of uncertainty for staff until the Children Bill received royal assent in November 2004.

Following transfer, responsibility for Cafcass Cymru lay with the Welsh Assembly. Cafcass Cymru was the name of the division of the Welsh Assembly government that discharged Cafcass functions.

Under the Children Act 2004, from April 2005 Cafcass functions in Wales became the sole responsibility of the Welsh Assembly. Section 38 of the Act also included provision for the assembly to request that HMICA inspect and report to it on:

- the discharge by the assembly of its functions concerning Cafcas in Wales
- the discharge by Welsh family proceedings officers of their function

A concordat between the Secretary of State for Constitutional Affairs an Lord Chancellor and the National Assembly for Wales in March 2005 se out further details about arrangements for HMICA inspection in Wales.

HMICA's July 2006 report 'Advisory and Support Services for Famil Proceedings in Wales' was based on fieldwork undertaken in January an

March 2006. The report was published in one volume in English and also with the entire Welsh translation included. It states:

> The period of transfer was a difficult and challenging time for the CAFCASS CYMRU management team. From early 2004 CAFCASS CYMRU became heavily involved with the Welsh Assembly Government in undertaking additional work related to the transfer. During this period, the Welsh Assembly provided supplementary resources to cover the costs of secondments, temporary appointments and a limited number of honorarium payments for certain postholders.

HMICA also stated:

> CAFCASS CYMRU is not a legal entity. Rather, it can be likened to a brand name for the service provided by the Assembly Government to children and families in family proceedings. CAFCASS CYMRU staff are now located within the Department for Social Justice and Regeneration (SJ&R) and the Chief Executive sits as one of the Department's Divisional Heads. The significant difference between CAFCASS CYMRU staff and other SJ&R staff is that the former are engaged in operational activities.

HMICA commented:

> At the time of the transfer, a number of issues had still to be addressed, including the structure of the organisation. CAFCASS CYMRU assumed responsibility for addressing those deficits post transfer and for assisting the Welsh Assembly Government to gain a necessary understanding of the implications of having responsibilities for CAFCASS functions. Its aim was to ensure that the Assembly could respond effectively to children, young people and their families as well as engage appropriately with key stakeholders.

The chief inspector's foreword explains: 'This report describes how well organisational change accompanying Cafcass devolution has been achieved. I am pleased that, overall, the many challenges have been met well and that service delivery without delay has been maintained. Inspectors also point to areas where wider improvements are needed and to wider changes affecting family justice where the Cafcass dimension will be crucial.'

The Office for Public Service Reform

With some links back to the government's 1999 White Paper Modernising Government,[23] the Prime Minister's Office for Public Service Reform

---

[23] https://www.civilservant.org.uk/library/1999_modernising_government.pdf

(OPRS) set out, in 2003, 10 principles with which inspectorates should comply. Its preamble included the following commitment to inspection:

> There are special accountabilities and standards attached to public money and the proper delivery of public services. Inspection makes an important contribution to the improvement of delivering public services and provides assurance on the stewardship of public resources ... the Government expresses its belief in the efficacy of targeted and user-focused inspection in providing assurance to the public and support for the improvement of public services.

As is discussed later, the principles set out below increasingly influenced the inspectorate's methodological approach to inspecting Cafcass.

i. The purpose of improvement. There should be an explicit concern on the part of inspectors to contribute to the improvement of the service being inspected. This should guide the focus, method, reporting and follow-up of inspection. In framing recommendations, an inspector should recognise good performance and address any failure appropriately. Inspection should aim to generate data and intelligence that enable departments more quickly to calibrate the progress of reform in their sectors and make appropriate adjustments.

ii. A focus on outcomes, which means considering service delivery to the end-users of the services rather than concentrating on internal management arrangements.

iii A user perspective. Inspection should be delivered with a clear focus on the experience of those for whom the service is provided, as well as on internal management arrangements. Inspection should encourage innovation and diversity and not be solely compliance-based.

iv. Proportionate to risk. Over time, inspectors should modify the extent of future inspection according to the quality of performance by the service provider. For example, good performers should undergo less inspection, so that resources are concentrated on areas of greatest risk.

v. Inspectors should encourage rigorous self-assessment by managers. Inspectors should challenge the outcomes of managers' self-assessments, take them into account in the inspection process and provide a comparative benchmark.

vi. Inspectors should use impartial evidence. Evidence, whether qualitative or quantitative, should be validated and credible.
vii. Inspectors should disclose the criteria they use to form judgements.
viii. Inspectors should be open about their processes, willing to take any complaints seriously, and able to demonstrate a robust quality-assurance process.
ix. Inspectors should have regard to value for money, their own included:
  - Inspection should look to see that there are arrangements in place to deliver the service efficiently and effectively.
  - Inspection itself should be able to demonstrate it delivers benefits commensurate with its cost, including the cost to those inspected.
  - Inspectorates should ensure they have the capacity to work together on cross-cutting issues, in the interests of greater cost effectiveness and reducing the burden on those inspected.
x. Inspectors should continually learn from experience, in order to become increasingly effective. This can be done by assessing their own impact on the service provider's ability to improve and by sharing best practice with other inspectors.

Inspectorate Methodologies

The following 14 short summaries illustrate some of the methodological approaches that were adopted by the inspectorates responsible for Cafcass inspections in the period between April 2001 and March 2007.

i. Notice – The inspectorate's proposed programme was shared with Cafcass well in advance and it never adopted an 'unannounced visit' approach sometimes used by other inspectorates for other services.
ii. Regional and thematic inspections – Inspections over several years covered all Cafcass' regions and also headquarters' functions. Thematic inspections were instead focused on single issues.
iii. Data collection and self-assessment – Inspections typically involved activity-related data collection from Cafcass, which was analysed in advance of fieldwork. Self- assessment by Cafcass was also a valuable tool.

iv. Meeting agendas – were increasingly circulated before face-to-face meetings. This helped to achieve a better focus and more efficient use of time and also encouraged a more thoughtful response to inspectors' questions.

v. Non-attributable comments – Reports on Cafcass rarely identified views or findings attributable to an individual but instead would refer to their generic role.

vi. Fast-tracking serious concerns – Where urgent action was needed by Cafcass before an inspection report was ready for publication, the issue would be immediately raised with senior management within Cafcass.

vii. Wider stakeholders – Inspectorate methodology included meeting with relevant stakeholders directly or inviting their written comments, or both. Depending on the focus of the inspection, stakeholders could include parents, solicitors, local authority senior managers and family judiciary. This approach worked less well with children the subject of proceedings.

viii. Gradings – Unlike some other inspectorates, the MCSI and HMICA did not grade Cafcass performance on a numerical scale (such as, 1- Requires immediate action to 5- Excellent) or with single-word judgements.

ix. Draft reports – Cafcass was invited to suggest any factual corrections to draft inspection reports before they were finalised for publication.

x. Recommendations – Unlike some other inspectorates, recommendations were usually aimed at helping Cafcass take identified steps to improve its services.

xi. Post-inspection reviews – Reports not only made recommendations but also published Cafcass' response, setting out what actions it would take and when. Inspectors followed these up in post-inspection review visits, reporting back to Cafcass by letter.

xii. Joint inspections – HMICA sometimes worked with other inspectorates on cross-cutting issues to examine how well different services worked individually and together. For example one involved domestic violence allegations and how these were addressed in proceedings by both HM Court Service and Cafcass; others focused on children's safeguarding.

xiii. Advisory Group – HMICA sometimes appointed an Advisory Group, as happened with the thematic inspection on the handling of domestic violence issues by Cafcass and HMCS, although the report stated: 'The views expressed in this Thematic Review are HMICA's and are not necessarily shared in full by the Advisory Group.'

xiv. Observers and secondees – HMICA occasionally invited a senior official from Cafcass' sponsoring department to accompany inspectors as an observer. This approach was also used with Ofsted when the Deputy Director Early Years joined an HMICA inspection six months before HMICA's move to the new Ofsted. After a careful selection process, secondees from Cafcass were occasionally engaged to be part of an Inspection team, but they were kept geographically well away from their normal regional location in Cafcass.

Unannounced Inspections

Notwithstanding what is said above at (i) about unannounced inspections of Cafcass, their use in other settings can be revealing in exposing what is really happening on the ground in contrast to what inspectors might be told elsewhere as the 'official line'.

For example, in 1998 a colleague and I were inspecting residential services for the elderly in a London local authority and were told by a headquarters manager that residents were washed and dressed about 8 am. But that was not so when we arrived one morning, unannounced, at 5 am. We found most up, dressed and wandering around. This turned out to be a 'deal' between night staff who finished at 7 am and day staff who followed. A manager was suspended.

In a boys' residential establishment having both secure and non-secure wings, I recall in the late 1980s making an unannounced early arrival during an inspection week:

I found the boys' bedrooms had been locked overnight in the non-secure wing in strict contravention of the statutory regulations and also while the night staff sat watching TV rather than undertaking their night patrols. I gave the head of the home a copy of the regulations – which he had never seen – and the bedroom locks were duly removed that morning.

Single Grade Descriptors

Although as mentioned above at (viii) single numerical grades were not used by the MCSI and HMICA, Ofsted was keen to introduce them within its proposed inspection methodology for Cafcass after 2007. I recall:

> *Attending an Ofsted senior management meeting in 2006 chaired by the new Ofsted chief inspector when this issue was discussed. I pointed out that Ofsted currently used two contradictory scales for inspections within its remit. For some services, one had the high figure meaning excellent, but for other services it meant poor. I said I would try to fit Cafcass in once this had been sorted out. The chief inspector said I was wrong, but fortunately her much more experienced deputy said I was right.*

Safeguarding Children

The government made a commitment in the 1998 White Paper *Modernising Social Services*[24] to put in place new arrangements to commission from all its chief inspectors of services involving children a joint report on children's safeguards. These reports would be produced every three years.

The first was published in October 2002[25] by the eight inspectorates,[26] with the Social Services Inspectorate in the lead. The report explains:

> The term safeguarding has not been defined in law or government guidance. It is a concept that has evolved from the initial concern about children and young people in public care to include the protection from harm of all children and young people and to cover all agencies working with children and their families.

The report continues:

> We have taken the term to mean:
>
> - all agencies working with children, young people and their families take all reasonable measures to ensure that the risks of harm to children's welfare are minimised; and
> - where there are concerns about children and young people's welfare, all agencies take all appropriate actions to address those concerns, working to agreed local policies and procedures in full partnership with other local agencies.

---

[24] Modernising Social Services: promoting independence, improving protection, raising standards, Cm 4169, London TSO, 1998

[25] https://www.justiceinspectorates.gov.uk/cjji/wp-content/uploads/sites/2/2014/04/safeguardingchildrenreport.pdf

[26] SSI, Probation, Crown Prosecution, Ofsted, Prisons, Health Improvement, Constabulary, MCSI

And it adds:

> We have included within this definition the responsibilities of agencies, particularly the police and probation services, in respect of potentially dangerous persons who present a risk of harm to the public, including children.

Each of the inspectorates offers a summary of relevant findings, examples of good practice and recommendations they made in their individual reports. Chapter 2 makes 30 recommendations addressed to different government departments and other agencies and organisations. Appendix B sets out eight standards and criteria. However, as with many reports – inspectorate or otherwise – there is a lingering doubt about the extent of their impact on their subject matter, especially when, as in this example, there are no arrangements in place to monitor the implementation of any inspectorate recommendations.

Changes in the Inspectorate Landscape

Writing in 2005,[27] I explain that the Chancellor of the Exchequer's budget statement in March 2005 sets out the public services inspectorate strategy:

> Its main aims are to:
> - Refocus inspection on what is relevant to people who use public services, the way they use them and the outcomes they experience
> - Rationalise, in order to simplify and manage better the complex pattern of multiple scrutiny that service providers experience and
> - Reduce the amount of inspection activity of approaches and burden generated and the variety that is a feature of having many similar bodies performing similar tasks.

In the same article, I also explain that in July 2005 the Department for Education and Skills (DfES) sets out its consultative proposals, *A Single Inspectorate for Children and Learners.*

> The aim is to bring together the children's work of the Commission for Social Care Inspection (CSCI), the CAFCASS inspection functions within HMICA, and the work currently undertaken by the Adult Learning Inspectorate (ALI) with the work of Ofsted. If the plans and legislative timetable are achieved, the merger with Ofsted may take effect from April 2007.

' 'So, what is the use of inspection?', Seen and Heard, Volume 15, Issue 4, Poyser, A.

The consultation ran for 14 weeks from 29 July to 4 November. In its response to the consultation, the government set out the remit for the new inspectorate as covering a number of sectors:

- Schools, including boarding, special and independent
- Further education and sixth-form colleges
- Local authority children's services
- Employers and work-based learning settings
- Social care providers, including the private, voluntary and community sectors
- Cafcass services
- Daycare and nursery education
- Childminding

The government response also laid out the benefits, including efficiencies and annual cost savings (£6.4m) based on an impact assessment summary published with the report, although it also anticipated there would be start-up, transitional costs (£13.5–19.5 million). Over the following months, Ofsted hosted a series of transitional planning meetings with the relevant inspectorates, and I attended on behalf of HMICA.

Joint Area Reviews (JARs)

The working relationship between HMICA and Ofsted started in 2004 as part of my role on the strategic and management boards led by Ofsted dealing with joint area reviews (JARs). Joint area reviews of children's services are carried out under section 20 of the Children Act 2004 and with accompanying regulations require:

> The Chief Inspector of Education, Children's Services and Skills, jointly with other relevant inspectorates, to review in a more effective and collaborative manner the effectiveness of local services and agencies in working together to protect and improve the well-being of children and young people.

The explanatory memorandum[28] says:

> They are necessary to deliver the Government's commitment (set out in the report *Tackling Child Sexual Exploitation*, March 2015) to deliver a new system of multi-agency reviews, to assess more effectively how local agencies

[28] https://www.legislation.gov.uk/uksi/2015/1792/pdfs/uksiem_20151792_en.pdf

> are working in a co-ordinated manner to protect children and young people. Inspectorates will be working together to assess a range of service provision, not just local authority services. Where a review has taken place, the Regulations therefore require the Chief Inspector ... to determine whether a written response is required to the report and, if so, from whom. This determination must be included in the report.
>
> Where the Chief Inspector has determined that a response is needed, all relevant agencies must co-operate in the production of the response so that it reflects the joint nature of the inspection. All of those agencies, including the local authority, must publish and make available on request a copy of both the report following the review and the written response.

New Ofsted

Following the proposals in the above reports and the White Paper *Higher Standards, Better Schools for All*[29,30] the inspectorate enlargement was achieved with the Education and Inspections Act 2006[31] receiving royal assent in November 2006, with implementation on 1 April 2007. I recall:

> Inspectors joining new Ofsted from HMICA and the other inspectorates were all appointed as HMIs (i.e. Her Majesty's Inspectors of Education, Children's Services and Skills). The statutory instrument[32] lists all their names – including mine – approved at a meeting of the Privy Council held with the Queen at Windsor Castle on 4 April 2007.

The legislation includes far more detail than comparable acts dealing with other inspectorates. Section 117 provides that the general purpose of the Office is to perform its functions to encourage 'the improvement of activities within the chief inspector's remit, the carrying on of those activities as user-focused activities, and the efficient and effective use of resources in the carrying out of those activities'.

In addition, in performing its functions, the Office is to have regard to the matters in subsection 2:

> (a) the need to safeguard and promote the rights and welfare of children;
> (b) views expressed by relevant persons about activities within the Chief Inspector's remit;
> (c) levels of satisfaction with such activities on the part of relevant persons;
> (d) the need to promote the efficient and effective use of resources in the carrying on of such activities;

Cm 6677, published on 25 October 2005

https://publications.parliament.uk/pa/cm200506/cmselect/cmeduski/633/633.pdf

https://www.legislation.gov.uk/ukpga/2006/40/notes/contents

SI 2007 No.1119

(e) the need to ensure that action by the Chief Inspector in relation to such activities is proportionate to the risks against which it would afford safeguards;
(f) any developments in approaches to inspection or regulatory action; and
(g) best practice amongst persons performing functions comparable to those of the Chief Inspector.

The wording of subsection 2(a) is of particular importance. It appears that this list is intended, as far as is possible, to reflect the government's 10 principles of public sector inspection referred to above – and to which I had drawn to Ofsted's attention at a much earlier meeting when the bill was being drafted. The 2006 Act also sets out inspection of Cafcass functions, powers of entry to its premises and to inspect documents.[33]

Although the organisation continues to be referred to as Ofsted as a convenient shorthand – and is familiar to the wider public by this name – the term does not form part of the 2006 legislation. Instead, it is a title carried forward from previous 1992 arrangements.[34] It is also often referred to in the media as a 'watchdog', which has other and, for many, less-complimentary connotations.

Concluding my article in *Seen and Heard* referred to earlier in this chapter, I note that since 2002 Cafcass has accepted all of the inspectorate's recommendations. My final comments are hopefully as true now as they were in 2005:

> As inspectors, we must always report as we find. This may be uncomfortable or inconvenient for CAFCASS, departments or ministers. But reports must always be professional, credible and have clear, evidence-based judgements that can stand up to scrutiny and challenge. Above all, they must make a positive difference.

Ofsted's First Annual Report

The chief inspector's first annual report under the Education and Inspection Act 2006 was published in November 2009[35] and states:

> Key Findings
>
> Overall, the pace of improvement in the Children and Family Court Advisory and Support Service (Cafcass) is too slow and the extent of change is

[33] Education and Inspections Act 2000, sections 143, 144 and 145

[34] The national scheme of inspections though a reconstituted HMI became known as the Office for Standards in Education (Ofsted) under the Education (Schools) Act 1992.

[35] https://assets.publishing.service.gov.uk/media/5a7c8ac7ed915d6969f459b7/0011.pdf

insufficient. Frontline practice is inconsistent so that minimum standards, including safeguarding, are not always met. However, Cafcass is taking seriously the scale of the improvements needed, and key strategic building blocks are being put in place. It has introduced good systems for managing the performance of its workforce and is tackling long-standing issues of accountability.

However, later the report also comments:

Positive steps have been taken by the Cafcass children's rights service to increase the involvement of children and young people in the work of Cafcass, particularly at a strategic level. The members of the Children and Young People's Board have produced impressive young inspectors' reports to help improve the service.

11

Departures

This chapter sets out some of the concerns that led to the departure of Cafcass' first chief executive and one board member. The relevant sources of information have been in the public domain for many years. The sole aim of this chapter is to illustrate the amount of time expended by the Cafcass chair, senior officials, ministers and MPs in dealing with the concerns. However, it should be stressed that no criticism of the conduct of either the chief executive or the board member is implied in this account.

Chief Executive

The difficult situation surrounding Cafcass' first chief executive took some time to resolve. It must inevitably have diverted important senior staffing and board resources away from what should have been other priorities. It must also have placed a considerable strain on an already under-resourced senior management team. And it also took up both Civil Service and parliamentary time.

In November 2001 Richard White wrote[1] 'The chief executive has been suspended from her post after several weeks on sick leave in 2001', adding that '*The Times* reported on 17 November that she was under investigation for an agreement in relation to a consultancy contract and a payoff for a senior executive'. But it was not until July 2002 that the matter was concluded.

On 26 July 2002, *The Guardian*[2] carried the headline 'Family Court Service Chief Executive Sacked After Row'.

The article included:

> The first public acknowledgement of problems in the service came when Lord Irvine told the Commons home affairs select committee three weeks before [the chief executive's] suspension: 'There are problems with the quality of management, and I do not want anything that I say to worsen a situation that exists.' He added: 'I am allocating no blame whatsoever, because this

[1] *New Law Journal*, 30 November 2001

[2] Family court service chief executive sacked after row | Children | The Guardian https://www.theguardian.com/society/2002/jul/26/childrensservices.childprotection

> is a very, very fraught situation for which none of us around this table would have liked to have been responsible.'

The article went on to say;

> David Cameron,[3] Conservative member of the select committee, said: 'It is wrong not to give taxpayers an explanation for the termination of [the chief executive's] contract, and it is typical how things like this happen just the day after parliament has gone into summer recess. This news has also emerged just two days after the permanent secretary to the lord chancellor's department appeared before our committee to give evidence. The lord chancellor's department should be open and frank about the problems with Cafcass and not try to sweep them under the carpet.

Sir Hayden Phillips, Permanent Secretary, LCD, vigorously denied Mr Cameron's remarks and wrote to the Home Affairs Committee, at which he had given oral evidence on 23 July in the following robust terms:[4]

> Press coverage of this event included comments attributed to a Committee member that suggested that this decision had been scheduled purposely to occur after my appearance at the Committee and after Parliament had risen. I would like to assure you this was not the case. A decision to dismiss the CAFCASS Chief Executive is a decision for the Board itself to make. The Chief Executive is its employee. There is no direct Ministerial role in this decision. Since CAFCASS had its own (acting) Accounting Officer, there was no direct role for me, as Principal Accounting Officer, in this process either.
>
> The Board reached its decision at one of its regular meetings, which had been scheduled several months in advance. I cannot comment on the reasons for her dismissal, as indeed I could not have done had I been asked at the Committee. I can, however, assure you that there was no manoeuvring of the timing of the decision, or the announcement, to make it after my appearance at the Committee or after Parliament had risen.

A Board Member's Concerns

This unfortunate series of events started early in 2001 and continued through to 2004. Relevant details are in the public domain and set out on the parliamentary website.[5,6]

MP for Witney (2001–2016); Prime Minister (2010–2016); Lord Cameron (recalled into government 13 November 2023)

https://publications.parliament.uk/pa/cm200102/cmselect/cmhaff/1143/2072313.htm

House of Commons - Constitutional Affairs - First Special Report (parliament.uk)

Select Committee on Constitutional Affairs First Special Report Protection of a witness – privilege, .3 January 2004.

Among those expressing concerns about the period prior to Cafcass' vesting day was one shadow board member who made extensive further criticisms once Cafcass became operational. She herself was roundly criticised for some of her actions. In her supplementary written evidence dated 2 May 2002 to the select committee, many serious shortcomings and tensions are alleged that at the time were difficult for the Cafcass chair and LCD officials to respond to adequately.

Initial Concerns

The board member first highlights[7] in writing to the select committee her concerns about the recruitment, selection and appointment of the board. She states that the closing date for applications for the chair and members of the board was 30 June 2000. Interviews for board members were held in September, but successful candidates were not informed until they received a letter of 10 January 2001.

> This delay in finalising our appointment prevented the Board from having any meaningful period as a shadow Board.

She then points out that although the LCD says that the reason for this was due to the delay and uncertainties of the legislation, she opines:

> While this may have made it difficult to finalise our full appointment, an interim temporary appointment could have been made, with an indication that full status was subject to the successful passage of the Bill. We could have been paid on a consultancy basis, which is the way we were in anyway [sic] paid prior to vesting day on 1 April 2001.

On selection, the board member was most surprised at the overall board composition, as she was expecting the majority of members to be 'heavyweights' from major stakeholder groups. Instead she found that:

> We were mostly intelligent and able people of a senior middle-management level rather light on relevant experience in the specific work of CAFCASS practitioners; setting up new organisations; running NDPBs; governing national service delivery and policy developing organisations; and budgets and finance, including the government approach.

And:

> Little attempt had been made to develop us into an effective team, to recognise and use our different skills and strengths or to acknowledge and remedy our weaknesses.

[7] House of Commons - Lord Chancellor's Department - Written Evidence (parliament.uk)

Despite the late appointment of the board, the board member says there appeared to be no hurry to get moving, and the first board meeting was only held on 13 February 2001, with no supporting papers. The first (and last) effective shadow board meeting was held on 9 March, three weeks before vesting day:

> Serious concerns were expressed and shown in the minutes:— there was nothing in the plan about the management and development of the Service. It would be necessary to define how the Service would be managed as a primary objective;— the plan was very 'light' on stakeholders needs;— the service was being operated outside the experience of the members of the Board;— the degree of independence (of practitioners) was being underestimated; and— a very real possibility of losing the support of Guardians.

The board member then states:

> We were in no position to hold the Management to account or to get relevant information for the organisation we were to take full responsibility for a few weeks later! We were quite unprepared as a group of people who had only just met and had varying and inadequate information. Furthermore, it appeared as if nothing was being expected of us. Surely, this has to be unacceptable.

The board member's written evidence about the shadow period outlines her next steps:

> I was so disconcerted by this laissez faire approach that I made arrangements to meet with the Chair, Chief Executive Designate and Project Manager prior in late February 2001 to clarify matters. I raised a number of concerns with the Chair and Project Director and these were brushed aside. I then attempted to organise an extra Board meeting prior to vesting day, but was prevented by the Chair, who postponed it to after vesting day. I discussed a number of governance concerns with the Chair, who asked me to put them in writing. My recommendations were largely supported in discussion at the next Board meeting and then appear to have been forgotten.

And:

> I was becoming increasingly concerned at the lack of preparedness of CAFCASS and the lack of awareness of the serious storm clouds brewing. I started to fear that as a Board we would be responsible but ineffective.

Continuing Concerns

The board member's concerns continued after vesting day on 1 April 2001, when she wrote to the select committee:

> From the start of CAFCASS it became clear that as a Board we were expected to rubber stamp the proposals of the Chief Executive, and this approach was supported by the Chair. Three members of the Board, Judge Fricker, Leonie Jordan and myself, became increasingly worried by the handling of the Guardian issue, but time and again we were opposed by the Chair, who was supporting the Chief Executive, and we were unable to persuade our colleagues to change direction. We wrote numerous papers and presented our arguments at the Board, but we made no headway.

She then states:

> Matters had got to such a state by early September 2001 that I wrote to the Lord Chancellor on 10 September 2001 outlining my concerns and suggesting a meeting. I indicated that Judge Fricker would be willing to join me in this meeting. We were called into the LCD and expected to meet with the Lord Chancellor. We were told there that he had read our letter and to be assured that action would be taken but he would not be meeting with us. Shortly after this, Judge Fricker resigned.

Such independent action was no doubt strongly disapproved of by the Cafcass chair and would have been judged as undermining both his authority and the board's wider corporate decision-making. On the other hand, many of the concerns might be considered valid but perhaps were not handled in the right way.

A Footnote

The select committee report adds a significant footnote:

> The model Code of Practice for NDPBs states that: 'Communications between the board and the minister will generally be through the chair. Nevertheless, any board member has the right of access to ministers on any matter which he or she believes raises important issues relating to his or her duties as a board member.'

More Evidence to the Committee

In June 2003 the Cafcass chairman submitted further supplementary written evidence to the select committee to counter some of what the board member had herself put in writing to it.[8] This said:

[8] House of Commons - Lord Chancellor's Department - Written Evidence (parliament.uk)

> The CAFCASS Board has seen a copy of the letter submitted to the Committee of 2 May 2003 (June) written by [the Board member] one of it's [sic] members. Following a discussion at its meeting on Tuesday, 17 June 2003, at which [the Board member] was present, the Board felt strongly that a short letter of clarification should be sent to the Committee. We do not think it would be helpful to cover each point made in the letter but the Board want to record that [the Board member's] letter was sent without any consultation with any other member of the Board. The letter does not reflect the view of other Board Members. The Board is concerned that the letter focuses on the past without sufficient acknowledgement of the significant progress and increasing forward momentum that has been established since December 2001. Other Board Members, or myself, are willing to contribute a different perspective on a range of issues [the Board member] refers to in her letter if the Committee would find this helpful.

Next Steps

The board member continued to serve as a board member until December 2003, when the Lord Chancellor, as is noted above, took the exceptional step of suspending her membership.[9]

In response to the Lord Chancellor's letter of 2 December to all board members, the board member replied on 3 December declining to resign. On 9 December the DfES Permanent Secretary spoke to all five board members who at that point had not resigned. By the following day, all but two board members had resigned, and by 11 December, one further board member had resigned. At that point there was only the one board member who had not done so.

The Lord Chancellor's Review

On 11 December the Lord Chancellor reviewed the situation and wrote at length to this remaining board member, who had not resigned, to suspend her, pending an examination of her personal conduct as a member of the board. His letter said:[10]

> Thank you for your letter of 3rd December 2003. I know that you have since had a meeting with David Normington, Permanent Secretary at the Department for Education and Skills. I understand that he asked you to reconsider my request that you should tender your resignation as a member of CAFCASS. I am sorry that you remain unwilling to do so. I remain of the

Op. cit. 248

House of Commons - Constitutional Affairs - First Special Report (parliament.uk) view that a fresh start is in the best interests of CAFCASS and the children and families it serves.

As David explained, my original request was based on Professor Sir Clive Booth's advice. At our request, he had conducted a fundamental review of the Board's membership. It was a 'central recommendation' of the Select Committee that this should be undertaken. Sir Clive advised that there should be a fresh start with the Board, and that all members of the Board should be invited to submit their resignations. You will be aware that I have now accepted resignations from 9 of your colleagues.

Given your unwillingness to resign, I have carefully considered the position and am minded to terminate your membership pursuant to Regulation 4(3)(b) of the CAFCASS (Membership, Committee and Procedure) Regulations 2000.

On 24th September 2003 the outgoing Chair, Anthony Hewson, made a recommendation to me that your membership should be terminated. He handed me a dossier detailing instances of alleged breach of your duties as a Board member with supporting documentary evidence. I asked a senior member of my Department with no previous involvement with CAFCASS to review this dossier. On 9 October 2003, he reported to me with his analysis of the dossier (below). I was giving careful consideration to these findings but decided to postpone further consideration of what action I should take because of the wider issues affecting the CAFCASS Board at that time. Mr Hewson ceased to be Chairman on 10 October, having tendered his resignation. On 16 October, I asked Sir Clive to conduct a review of the membership of the Board, as recommended by the Select Committee. As you now know, I then accepted Sir Clive's advice that all Board members should be invited to tender their resignations. While these events were unfolding, I did not consider it sensible simultaneously to pursue the separate matter of your personal conduct as a member. Given your unwillingness to resign in company with your colleagues of the old Board, I have now had to review the situation.

I am satisfied that there is evidence that you have:
i. failed to behave in a corporate manner;
ii. behaved inappropriately in relation to the Chief Executive and staff of CAFCASS;
iii. refused to observe confidentiality.

If established, the case could justify termination of your membership of the Board. Before making any final decision, I would welcome your comments on this matter. In the meantime, I am suspending your membership of the Board with immediate effect. During your suspension you will not receive any Board papers and will not be entitled to attend any Board meetings. You

> must not enter CAFCASS premises. During the period of your suspension, you will receive payment equivalent to the fee that you would receive for 3.5 days' work per month. I invite you to provide me with your comments in writing on the above matters by close of play on 16 January 2004. Once I have had the opportunity to consider your written comments, I will consider whether (a) to terminate your membership; or (b) to lift the suspension of your membership.
>
> I would ask you to indicate in writing by 5.00pm on 12 December that you consent to the terms of your suspension. You should be aware that if you do not consent to the terms of your suspension, I will have no alternative but to terminate your membership of the Board with immediate effect. If, of course, you prefer not to engage with the process outlined above, I remain willing to accept your resignation.

Suspension

On 12 December the board member wrote to the Lord Chancellor consenting to the terms of her suspension.

Another Select Committee's Interest

The Constitutional Affairs First Special Report was published on 13 January 2004[11] addressing the subject 'Protection of a Witness – Privilege'. It summarised the events surrounding the suspended board member and annexed a volume of additional documentation.

The committee's conclusions state:

> In the view of the Committee, the process of dealing with the complaints against [the suspended Board member], starting with the dossier prepared by Mr Hewson, continuing with the review of the matter by Mr Crawley and ending with the letter from the Lord Chancellor to [the Board member] and the supporting document might be regarded as a prima facie breach of privilege. Accordingly, we believe that the House should refer this matter to the Committee on Standards and Privileges.

And Finally

On 21 January 2004 the Secretary of State wrote to the suspended board member apologising for not making it clear that her suspension was not connected to the fact of her giving evidence to the select committee. There was also some media coverage of these later developments.[12,13]

---

[11] House of Commons - Constitutional Affairs - First Special Report (parliament.uk)

[12] https://www.independent.co.uk/news/uk/politics/falconer-guilty-of-contempt-for-attacking-whistleblower-54270.html

[13] BBC NEWS | Politics | MPs back witness sacking probe

An Afterthought

The details set out above were of concern to many people. Arguably, they must have made the operation of the board over a long period very difficult. One wonders whether, for example, at such a critical time in Cafcass' post-vesting-day operations, it was possible for the board's urgent business to have been conducted in a cordial, constructive and trusting atmosphere.

12

Two Questions

This short chapter discusses two alternative hypothetical scenarios about decisions that might have been made between 1998 and 2001. These are what might have happened had welfare support services not been unified and whether a longer transitional period for establishing Cafcass might have been possible.

Retaining the Status Quo

Among key influences that led to Cafcass being established were the ambitions of the New Labour government in 1997, commitment within the Civil Service, encouragement of the family judiciary and broad support for the concept, at least in principle, from across most of the professional field.

Although at paragraph 1.31 the consultation paper argued 'in a very real sense, change is not optional', it went on to explain that 'the government is committed to wide-ranging reform' and also stressed that 'the present court welfare arrangements are not in crisis. Rather, it is the longer-term advantages that might accrue from a unified service that need to be considered.' It further pointed out that 'the rationalisation of the organisational arrangements under one government department would allow great flexibility in the deployment of resources' and 'where savings can be made, these offer opportunities to enhance the overall service'. It concluded that 'the proposals ... need to be placed within the wider agenda for change and the potential that may flow from it'.

But had these factors been ignored or overridden, the status quo in the delivery of welfare support services might have continued to operate. This could have arisen at the political and parliamentary levels had the enabling legislation not successfully completed all its parliamentary stages and been 'lost' by the end of the parliamentary session in late November 2000, as indeed nearly happened, as mentioned in an earlier chapter. Alternatively, to maintain the 'no change' option, minor legislative adjustments to the bill would have been needed to allow for the family court welfare functions to be incorporated into the new proposed National Probation Service (NPS).

For example, clause 1(3) of the Criminal Justice and Court Services Bill had regulation-making powers about the purposes of the National Probation Service. These could have included a provision to add among the NPS functions a service to be made available locally for welfare reporting under section 7 of the Children Act 1989 on issues around separation and divorce involving children and in certain adoption proceedings. FCWs would have continued their work from offices within the probation estate and on unchanged pay scales. While maintaining an ongoing supply of qualified and experienced staff would have been challenging in a post-2001 criminal justice organisation that was intended neither to be social-work-orientated nor child-focused, perhaps with careful attention, meeting this welfare function might not have been impossible to achieve.

Both the widely respected work of the children's branch of the Official Solicitor (OS) and the 59 Galro panels covering England and Wales might have been maintained within the range of delivery mechanisms then operating. Local tax arrangements for self-employed Galro panel members would have remained undisturbed. Both the Official Solicitors children's branch and Galro services would have continued to be linked to their respective government departments and ministers. A great deal of departmental expenditure – perhaps millions of pounds – could have been saved and redirected towards front-line service improvements. And of great importance, the high levels of stress experienced by so many that accompanied the setting up and early implementation of Cafcass would surely have been avoided.

However, whether the continuation after 2001 of welfare support services in their former arrangements would have survived possibl scrutiny as part of the 2011 Family Justice Review seems unlikely.

A Longer Period of Transition

Turning to the second hypothetical scenario, the question posed whether there could have been a longer period of transition pre-Cafcas If the integration of welfare support services was not to be denied, we the declared departmental reasons advanced for not allowing a mo realistic period of time between the four months from royal assent on

November 2000 and commencement on 1 April 2001 – as had been strongly advised in the 1998 consultation paper – entirely convincing or impossible to resolve?

A longer period of transition might have allowed a Cafcass board to better understand its own role as part of the NDPB; address service demands such as concerns about delay; as well as better plan to meet ambitious departmental expectations and requirements. A painful judicial review about self-employed guardians might have been avoided, as might also the hugely time-consuming and long drawn-out processes around the one board member's departures. Many of the other difficulties evidenced by the 2003 select committee might have been forestalled, avoided or more effectively addressed.

The select committee said[1] that the decision to proceed on a foreshortened timetable was a serious misjudgement:

> The Government should not have allowed the timetable for the establishment of the National Probation Service to dictate the unrealistic programme for the establishment of CAFCASS. The decision to do so makes CAFCASS appear of secondary importance. The impression was gained that the Departmental priorities of the Lord Chancellor's Department were secondary to those of the Home Office. It is vital that all Government Ministers give priority to work with children in line with their commitments under the UN Convention on the Rights of the Child.

The government's robust response to these criticisms is set out in its October 2003 report:

> Our evidence acknowledged that the time available for the establishment of CAFCASS was less than ideal and all involved would have valued more time being available for further development. This did not, however, reflect any lack of priority to CAFCASS.

The government next argued that:

> It was important to develop CAFCASS to the same timetable as that for the establishment of National Probation Service (NPS), since the staff involved in both changes were then part of the same workforce.

ts response continued:

> At the time leading up to establishment of these bodies, staff had to choose which of the new organizations to transfer to. Putting either of the putative organisations on different establishment timetables could have been very

House of Commons - Committee on the Lord Chancellor's Department - Third Report (parliament.uk)

> unsettling for staff, and in particular for CAFCASS had it been delayed since prospective staff would have been asked to transfer to an organization that did not formally exist.
>
> And ... putting both organisations on the same but extended establishment timetable was not possible due to the wider changes around the creation of the NPS. Attempting to do so could have been equally unsettling for staff and stakeholders, including the staff of the other services that were planned to transfer into CAFCASS, such as the guardians and from the Official Solicitor, as they would have been left in a prolonged period of uncertainty. The planned timetable for establishment of CAFCASS was foreshortened by the delay in receiving Royal Assent to the Criminal Justice & Court Services Act.

As is often found in other legislation, the Criminal Justice and Court Services Bill 2000 had a provision at clause 20 allowing the act 'to come into force on such days as the Lord Chancellor or the Secretary of State may by order appoint'. It also said that different days may be appointed for different purposes and different areas.

Arguably, most if not all the 'difficulties' alluded to above in the October 2003 government response might have been addressed and successfully overcome within an extended transitional period, especially if driven by political will, a well-prepared plan, clearer communications and skilled leadership – and skilled leadership includes consulting with and involving key practitioners, many more of whom if handled more sensitively might have opted to join Cafcass, albeit on revised terms and conditions.

Setting the commencement date for the National Probation Service for 1 April 2001 was seemingly driven more by departmental and ministerial considerations and less about children and families as users of family courts at a fraught time in their lives. Some might also share a view that ministers are not immune to a strong desire to 'get results on their watch' – and also perhaps before a cabinet reshuffle.

13

Past and Future

The final chapter of this book offers some reflections about Cafcass and family justice within a wider context and timescale.

Government Mistakes

In introducing their book *The Blunders of our Government,*[1] King and Crewe tell a variety of blunder-related horror stories, adding that 'our stories are worth telling in their own right' before cautioning that 'governments of all parties appear equally blunder-prone – a fact that itself suggests that there are systematic defects in the British system of government, defects rooted in the culture and institutions of Whitehall and Westminster having little to do with party leaders, party members or partisan ideologies'.[2]

The Guardian review of this book said:[3]

> Some of them are widely remembered, such as the poll tax, the Millennium Dome and membership of the Exchange Rate Mechanism, others almost forgotten, such as individual learning accounts and the Assets Recovery Agency. A few, such as Labour's comically bungled distribution of European Union subsidies to British farmers under a new 'single payment' scheme, were scarcely noticed even at the time. In all these instances, ministers failed wholly to achieve the outcome they intended; sometimes they achieved the opposite. They also, in several cases, wasted billions of pounds of public money and did great damage, sometimes lethal damage, to the people they were supposedly trying to help.

Had both authors still been alive in 2024, a second edition updating their book would surely have had a rich range of potential source material.

As King and Crewe might have suggested, Cafcass' early history is also a story worth telling in its own right. This book offers such an opportunity. It is worth remembering that in the period 2001–2002, and despite many Cafcass-related and wider family justice problems across England and

The Blunders of our Governments, King, A. and Crewe, I., Oneworld Publications, 2013
Ibid. page xi
The Blunders of our Governments by Anthony King and Ivor Crewe – review | Politics books | The uardian 4 September 2013

Wales, hundreds of children involved in family proceedings continued to receive a service that, at least at a broad level, reflected the standards of front-line practice of the former three welfare support services operating in 1999–2000. Even so, as discussed in several earlier chapters, there were service weaknesses as well, and in a few places more serious failures. Bearing these in mind and also taking account of budgetary issues, arguably Cafcass' early years should not be fairly judged as 'a blunder' of policy in the way described by these authors.

The period of preparation for Cafcass, followed by its implementation, were without doubt for many crisis-ridden. They also exacted a very heavy personal toll on a number of the professionals most closely involved. The ongoing concerns about delay in proceedings across the wider family justice system at that time, and for which Cafcass accepted some responsibility, must also have had an inevitable, negative and regrettable impact on the very children that were meant to be the primary focus and priority – and, as well, their wider families.

Given the history leading up to Cafcass and into its early years, which has been laid out in earlier chapters, there will be some voices of discontent – probably a minority – who continue to maintain that welfare support services were seriously flawed up to April 2001 and continued to be so thereafter.

Such criticism may reach beyond Cafcass and be addressed to the entire family justice system.

Other accounts about Cafcass' early years may help assess the balance of the organisation's strengths and weaknesses – and place them alongside emerging contemporary challenges that both it and the wider family justice system are certain to have to face for years to come.

The story around the development of the family justice system so far is multi-faceted and complex. Some events occur consecutively; others concurrently. Which factors directly influence other elements is often hard – indeed sometimes impossible – to fathom with certainty. This was probably true throughout all the post-World War period touched on in this book. And it often does not appear to be any easier trying to fit the pieces together with the benefit of hindsight.

Comparisons

Looking more widely across this period, questions might be posed, such as:

- Are there other examples of other major public service reorganisations undertaken about that time that experienced major difficulties?
- If so, are they in any way comparable to the reform of welfare support services?
- Can any broader lessons be learnt that might be of interest across a wider public policy audience?

Some might argue that each situation is likely to have more elements of difference than factors in common, thus rendering any attempted 'read across' comparison invalid. But imagine leaving that objection to one side for a moment; it might be relevant at least to ask how the reorganisation of the National Probation Service (NPS) fared under the same founding legislation as for Cafcass with the Criminal Justice and Court Services Act 2000 and its implementation in April 2001.

As far as broad policy is concerned, while Cafcass has had no major legislative changes imposed on it to date, other than devolving part of its service to the Welsh Assembly in April 2005, the NPS experienced several. What Cafcass has experienced are a number of useful policy and practice protocols developed with the Family Division and organisations such as the Association of Directors of Children's Services (ADCS). Other changes are in family court rules as well as rule changes to take account of new legislation, such as, for example, the Family Law Act.

For the NPS as one example, the Offender Management Bill, introduced in Parliament late in 2006, was intended to enable probation areas to become trusts as part of wider government policy to open up the provision of correctional services to greater competition from the voluntary, community and private sectors. This followed one of the recommendations of the Carter Report (2003). Other changes were to introduce a system of 'end-to-end offender management', with one named offender manager having responsibility for an offender throughout his or her sentence (be it in custody, the community or both), and to 'rebalance sentencing' in order to redress the drift towards less and less serious offences resulting in imprisonment or community sentences.

House of Commons Justice Committee

Further evidence of government-imposed policy shifts on the NPS is provided by the House of Commons Justice Committee, which reported at length on the role of the Probation Service in July 2011. Its conclusions state[4] that 'the Probation Service has been through a decade of change – from the setting up of a national service, through the development of NOMS,[5] to the establishment of trusts – and more change is yet to come'.

A Note of Caution

Writing in May 2001,[6] I conclude:

> Any objective look at social issues in Britain would recognise that there are still huge problems of inequality of opportunity. The wealth gap widens inexorably and aspects of the social structure are clearly under strain; indeed, so too are some of the physical ones. On the eve of the first general election of the twenty-first century,[7] we survey our malfunctioning public transport systems, congested roads, a rising London water table, polluted rivers and beaches, large tracts of countryside devastated by this year's foot and mouth outbreak, unprecedented floods and the latest 'race' riots in Oldham.

Even though some of these issues strike a familiar chord a quarter of a century later in 2024, surely one would be mistaken to assume that nothing will change in family justice and Cafcass in the future. A more likely course is to anticipate that change is inevitable – and if so, among the hard, ongoing challenges that will always remain are those of predicting with a degree of confidence what may be different, when and why.

Many would argue that the wider family justice system is beset with challenging issues, of which many have been major difficulties for decades. The longstanding issue of delay in the duration of some family proceedings arising from the interaction of a range of factors – whether locally, regionally or nationally – is but one example. Another is the imprecise application of 'risk management' as part of the proper aim of trying with all possible professional skill to assess future welfare for a child – and the disastrous, perhaps even fatal, consequences of making a mistake.

---

4 https://publications.parliament.uk/pa/cm201012/cmselect/cmjust/519/519i.pdf

5 National Offender Management Service

6 Op. cit. 6

7 7 June 2001

The Modern World

Rapid technological advances have affected all walks of life and their institutions in today's modern world. We have significantly moved from a paper-orientated basis for doing business to a range of electronic documentation and communication devices. The Covid pandemic further developed use of these, including, for example, virtual meetings coupled with increased home-working.

The wider political background may also remind us that over the period that is the main focus covered by this book, the Conservatives were in power from 1979 to 1997; Labour from 1997 to 2010; the Conservative–Liberal Democrat coalition from 2010 to 2015; and the Conservatives again since 2015. Throughout all these years there has been a variable economic climate characterised by periods of growth followed by others of austerity – familiarly known as 'boom and bust'. But financial factors span a global stage. Once a giant financial institution such as Lehmann Brothers is allowed to fail, others follow in what can be termed 'the domino effect'. All this occurred over one weekend in October 2008 and was part of the wider financial crisis.

These factors have inevitably affected levels of investment in public services. Even so, it is perhaps fortunate that much – but by no means all – of what I was personally involved with, as described in some previous chapters, took place when departmental funding often seemed quite generous. Inside knowledge of the 'ways and means' of securing funding may also have played an important part in furthering what were judged as departmental and/or wider government priorities.

Another factor is the debatable proposition that family law and linked welfare and legal services have rarely, if ever, featured among the highest of any government's priorities. This may be in part because they are not generally seen as areas of public policy that have readily attracted voters to one or another of the UK's main political parties whether at a general election or in local ones.

Assessing Costs and Value

The overall annual cost of family proceedings dealt with by the family justice system – whether in 2001 or today – is nigh impossible to calculate with any degree of certainty. Instead, broad estimates and assumptions may have to suffice. Such an assertion is mainly based on the challenges of agreeing definitions about the system's core elements of funding, whether from central and local government, the voluntary sector or elsewhere, including those deriving from associated peripheral aspects, such as the range of experts or conciliation services. To running costs would have to be added an element for depreciation of estates and equipment, as well taking into account income from court application fees and any awarded costs.

Although an exact figure may not be known, the overall amount possibly totals several hundred million pounds annually for England alone at current prices. One may question where the traditional '3 E's' concept of efficiency, effectiveness and economy fit alongside other important policy directives, such as achieving better long-term outcomes for the children who are the subject of family proceedings. Against such a complex background, this book remains neutral, as it is unable to present evidence in support of any claim that the current system does, or indeed does not, offer value for money.

Further Reflections

Writing in 2010 to mark the Children Act 1989 – 21 Years On,[8] Brenda Hale (then Justice of the Supreme Court) explained:

> The Law Lords (now the Supreme Court Justices) only take those cases that involve a 'point of law of general public importance'. They are looking at the big picture rather than its everyday application in the courts. So, it is quite a surprise that they have decided so many cases about the *Children Act* 1989 in the nearly two decades since it came into force. It is a salutary lesson to those of us whose mission was to simplify and clarify the law.
>
> We tried to foresee the impact of the European Convention on Human Rights, but we did not then envisage the Convention rights might become part of the law of the UK (through the *Human Rights Act* 1988. We did not foresee the influx of child asylum-seekers for whom the local authorities would have to take responsibility. And we could not foresee all the real life problems that would come along to tax the principles that we had devised and the words that the draftsman had used to enact them.

And she continued:

> The cases decided in the highest courts fall into our broad categories:
>
> - those exploring the application of the welfare principle in new or unusual situations

[8] Op. cit. 49

- those exploring the meaning of the threshold criteria and the courts' powers in care proceedings
- those considering the scope of local authorities' powers and duties towards children in need
- those considering the very nature of proceedings under the Act.

These are, of course, the most fundamental questions of principle raised by the Act. They mainly concern the powers and duties of local children's services authorities in public law; more mundane questions of private law have stayed in the lower courts.

Concluding

In looking to the future from a 2024 standpoint, what new developments may be viewed by many as progress should always require careful prior scrutiny because some decisions labelled well-meaning and considered posing low risk at the point when they are taken might later lead to significant actions – for example, at a legal, policy or practice level. The risk is that earlier decisions may prove later to have important – although unintended – negative consequences.

Foresight is not perfect; hindsight is a powerful tool – and it can be unforgiving in its judgement. Two current public inquiries yet to report may demonstrate this again. The first may be the Grenfell Tower Inquiry, which was created to examine the circumstances leading up to and surrounding the fire at Grenfell Tower on the night of 14 June 2017, killing more than 70 people. A second may be the UK Covid-19 Inquiry, which was set up in 2023 to examine the UK's response to and impact of the Covid-19 pandemic, and learn lessons for the future.

The evolving legal framework governing family justice, including the work of Cafcass, within the wider context of obligations under domestic law and key international conventions, requires that the many professional disciplines concerned always continue to strive to do their best and work together effectively. Sometimes organisational cultures and rivalries can undermine such efforts.

Despite its many difficulties, dilemmas and challenges – historical and ongoing – the family justice world has seemingly sufficiently attractive – indeed magnetic – qualities that for many years have been highly motivating for the numerous professionals who opt to continue to work within it.

Long may that scenario continue …

Appendix One

Cafcass' First Board Membership

As described in the Lord Chancellor's Department press notice.

His Honour Judge Nigel Fricker QC: Nigel has been a Circuit Judge since 1984; Care Centre designated Family Judge since 1991. He is electing to take early retirement in order to serve on the Board. He was a member of Family Proceedings Rule Committee from 1997 to 2001. He is General editor, "Emergency Remedies in the Family Courts" 1989-1999; Consulting Editor, "Emergency Remedies" since 1999 and "Family Court Practice" since 1991.
Peter Hargrave: holds an accountancy qualification, but much of his recent work has been in general management. Board experience in the public, private and independent sectors; Managing Director of the Flagship Housing Group until April 2000. Currently works as a management consultant and sits on the Boards of an NHS Trust and a special Housing Association for autistic people. He lives in Norwich with his wife, Denise. He has two adult children.
Leonie Jordan: a solicitor whose experience is primarily in the child care field. She has practised in local government, private practice and in the voluntary sector. In recent years, she has concentrated on developing training and workshops for child care professionals on law and practice issues and provided advice to local authorities on procedures and practice developments. She has also worked in the voluntary sector to promote participation by children and their families in the making of decisions affecting them.
Angela M. Killick: Angela is a former civil servant with the research councils and Department of the Environment. She was subsequently chai for ten years of three NHS Health Authorities and Trusts. She has been local councillor for many years including chair of social services; ha extensive experience with voluntary organisations. Angela is a former JI former member and chair of children's charity running eleven mixe economy nurseries in central London and chair of governors, loc

primary school. She is married, with one teen-age son and an extended step-family.

Anne Morgan OBE JP: Joined the National Association of Citizens Advice Bureaux in 1974 from a marketing background with Unilever. Co-founded NACAB North Wales in 1975. Served as the North Wales Area Officer from 1982 to 1995, successfully pioneering holistic advice services via inter-agency collaboration. Appointed Director NACAB Wales in 1995, responsible for strategic services to 137 CABx and member of the Corporate Management Team charged with the strategic direction of services to CABx across England and Wales.Served a member of the National Assembly for Wales Voluntary Sector Partnership Council. In 1999 was awarded OBE for services in Wales. Member of Welsh Consumer Council. Vice-Chair of the North Wales Agricultural Wages Board. Appointed a magistrate to the Denbighshire Bench in November 2000. Anne took an early retirement from NACAB in October 2000 to pursue new interests, including management consultancy services for the "not for profit" sector.

Pip O'Byrne: Pip works for the London Borough of Camden as an Assistant Director in the Leisure and Community Services Department where she has a diverse management portfolio which includes the Play, Sports and Physical Activity Services. She is also a member of the Council's corporate strategic management teams for Children's Services, Community Safety, Youth Crime, Anti Social Behaviour, Regeneration and Health. Pip is chair of Kids Club Network, the national organisation promoting the development of out of school play and care clubs for children aged 4-14 years. Pip has spent most of her professional life working on children, family and community issues. She is a member of he Childcare Commission.

Nalini Varma: Qualified social worker with extensive experience of management in the voluntary sector. Formerly Chief Executive of the Rainer Foundation - a young people's charity. Trustee of two grant-making organisations. Recently appointed lay member of the Criminal njuries Compensation Appeals Panel. Born in South Africa. Lives in ondon with husband and children.

Mike Walker: Mike started work in Durham Children's Department in 967. For the next 26 years, he worked for a number of Local Authorities in various positions before taking the opportunity of early retirement from his last post as Assistant Director of Social Services (Disabilities). This enabled him to develop his interests in the disability movement and to work with individuals in an advocacy role. He is currently working as a project co-ordinator for a Black Disability Group in Kirklees and is currently investigating the needs of young disabled people leaving the educational system.He also works as an independent consultant with a particular interest in developing opportunities for disabled people to enter higher education and the professions. He lectures occasionally on employment law and disability, and has carried out research for CCETSW. Mike is an active member of the Social Care Association (SCA) whose aim is to promote best practice.

Nedine Watson-Cutts: Nedine is a qualified social worker and has worked primarily in South East London Boroughs in community and statutory social work settings for the past 15 years.She currently manages the Adolescence Services in the London Borough of Bromley Social Services Department. She has previously managed childcare teams, a hospital social work team and developed Leaving care and After care services. She is keen to involve service users, especially young people, in service and policy development and to ensure that issues of diversity are addressed.

Judy Weleminsky: is a management consultant specialising in the voluntary and not for profit sectors. She has extensive managemen experience having been chief executive of three major national voluntary organisations, most recently the National Council for Voluntary Organisations from 1991 to 1994 and prior to that the Nationa Schizophrenia Fellowship. She has a masters degree in Organisationa Psychology, lives in London and has two young children.

Cafcass' Second Board Membership

As described at the time on the Cafcass website.

Baroness Pitkeathley OBE was appointed Chair of CAFCASS in 2004, i 2005 she also took on the role of Chair of the Home Office Advisory Pan on Futurebuilders. Jill is currently President of Volunteering Englan Community Council for Berkshire and The Prostate Cancer Charity. Sh is Vice President of Carers UK and the Princess Royal Trust for Carer She was raised to the peerage in 1997, sits on the Labour benches and is very active working peer.

Gillian Baranski Justices' Chief Executive on the South Wales Magistrates' Courts Committee, and a barrister. She was formerly Clerk to the Cardiff Justices/Chief Legal Advisor to the Cardiff Justices and has over 20 years' experience of Family Courts.

Jennifer Bernard Consulting Director at City and Guilds, Jennifer has previously been Director of Services for Children and Young People, NSPCC, Chief Executive of the Central Council for Education and Training in Social Work and Director of Social Services at Newcastle Upon Tyne City Council.

Margo Boye-Anawoma A barrister specialising in children law. She is also a Deputy District Judge of the Principal Registry of the Family Division in London and a committee member of the Joseph Rowntree Charitable Trust.

Erica De'Ath OBE Previously Chief Executive of the National Council of Voluntary Child Care Organisations, Chief Executive of the National Stepfamily Association and the Foundation for the Study of Infant Deaths. Erica is currently a Trustee of the National Children's Bureau, and the National Council for Voluntary Organisations and has published widely on family and children's issues.

Mark Eldridge Director of Legal Operations, Greater London Magistrates' Courts Authority and a barrister. He was formerly Chair of the Association of Justices' Chief Executives before taking up his present post.

Baroness Howarth of Breckland OBE Former Chief Executive of ChildLine she also worked for many years at Chief Officer and Assistant Chief Officer level in social services departments. She serves on the Board of the Food Standards Agency, is Trustee of a number of Children's charities and a patron of the National Youth Advocacy Scheme. She was vice-chair of the National Care Standards Commission and is secretary to the All Parliamentary Children's Group.

Harry Marsh A member of the General Social Care Council and a freelance consultant. He was Chief Executive of Contact a Family, and he was previously an Assistant Director of Family Service Units. He is a Trustee and Vice Chair of the National Children's Bureau.

Richard Sax A family law solicitor and partner at Manches. He is a Deputy District Judge of the Principal Registry of the Family Division. He is a founder member and former Chair of the Solicitors Family Law

Association, and has been a member of its Children Committee since its inception.

Judith Timms OBE An independent consultant and former Chief Executive of the National Youth Advocacy Service. She is a Hon research fellow in the Faculty of Law at the University of Liverpool and a Vice President of the Family Mediators Association. An experienced Guardian ad Litem, her publications include "Manual of Practice Guidance for Guardians ad Litem and Reporting Officers.

Professor Jane Tunstill A Visiting Professor of Social Work at Kings College, London, Jane previously held Chairs of Social Work at Keele University and Royal Holloway, London University. She has worked in the voluntary and statutory child care sectors, and undertaken a wide range of commissioned research studies of services for children and families.

Nicholas Stuart CB - Co-opted Board member Former Principal Finance Officer for DfEE and now retired from the Civil Service, Nicholas Stuart is Chair of Governors at Edward Wilson Primary School and a Trustee of Harrow Mission. During a distinguished civil service career he was Private Secretary to the Head of the Civil Service and the Prime Minister, and a member of the Cabinet of the President of the European Commission. In DfEE he was Director General for Employment and Lifelong Learning, and Director General for Lifelong Learning.

Appendix Two

The Lord Chancellor's Advisory Committee on Judicial Case Management in Public Law Children Act cases (2003)

The Honourable Mr Justice Munby (Chair)
The Honourable Mr Justice Coleridge (Chair)
His Honour Judge Cryan
Senior District Judge Angel, Principal Registry of the Family Division
District Judge Harrison CBE (Association of District Judges)
District Judge Rawkins (Association of District Judges)
District Judge (Magistrates' Courts) Crichton
Ernest Ryder QC
Mark Camley, Court Service
Bruce Clark, Department of Health
Audrey Damazer, Justices' Clerks' Society
Nigel Druce, Association of Directors of Social Services
Julia Eeles, Association of Justices' Chief Executives
Christine Field JP, Magistrates' Association
Sally Field, Lord Chancellor's Department
Katherine Gieve, Solicitors Family Law Association
Liz Goldthorpe, Association of Lawyers for Children
Jane Held, Association of Directors of Social Services
Derek Hill, Public Legal Services Division, Lord Chancellor's Department
Sheri Holland, Child Care Law Joint Liaison Group
Elaine Laken, Justices' Clerks' Society
Elizabeth Lawson QC, FLBA
Angela Nield, Association of Lawyers for Children
Andrew MacFarlane QC, Family Law Bar Association
Pat Monro, The Law Society
Charles Prest, Cafcass
Rachel Rogers, The Law Society
Philip Thomson, Child Care Law Joint Liaison Group
John Briden, Lord Chancellor's Department
Emran Mian, Lord Chancellor's Department
Dave Berry, Lord Chancellor's Department (Secretary)

Author

Arran Poyser worked in residential care for children and young people, the subject of the formerly named juvenile court proceedings and later in two London probation and after-care services with adult offenders. He then held senior management posts for 15 years in three London social services departments. In 1985 he was appointed to the Social Services Inspectorate at the Department of Health and Social Security (DHSS).

Among his responsibilities in London and nationally were contributing to many activities linked to the Children Act 1989 and providing sustained support to the guardian ad litem services across England and Wales. He was closely involved in the preparation of the 1998 consultation paper *Support Services in Family Proceedings: Future Organisation of Court Welfare Services* and was later seconded to the Lord Chancellor's Department to help establish the Children and Family Court Advisory and Support Service (Cafcass) in April 2001.

Arran Poyser was appointed to the Magistrates' Courts Service Inspectorate (MCSI) to have director responsibility for its new statutory duty to inspect Cafcass, retaining this role when MCSI later became HM Inspectorate of Court Administration (HMICA) and subsequently when this duty was transferred to the Office for Standards in Education, Children's Services and Skills (Ofsted), newly created in 2007.

Arran Poyser's inspectorate responsibilities for Cafcass in England ended in 2008 when he retired from Ofsted.

Milton Keynes UK
Ingram Content Group UK Ltd.
UKHW022334300824
1450UKWH00023B/372